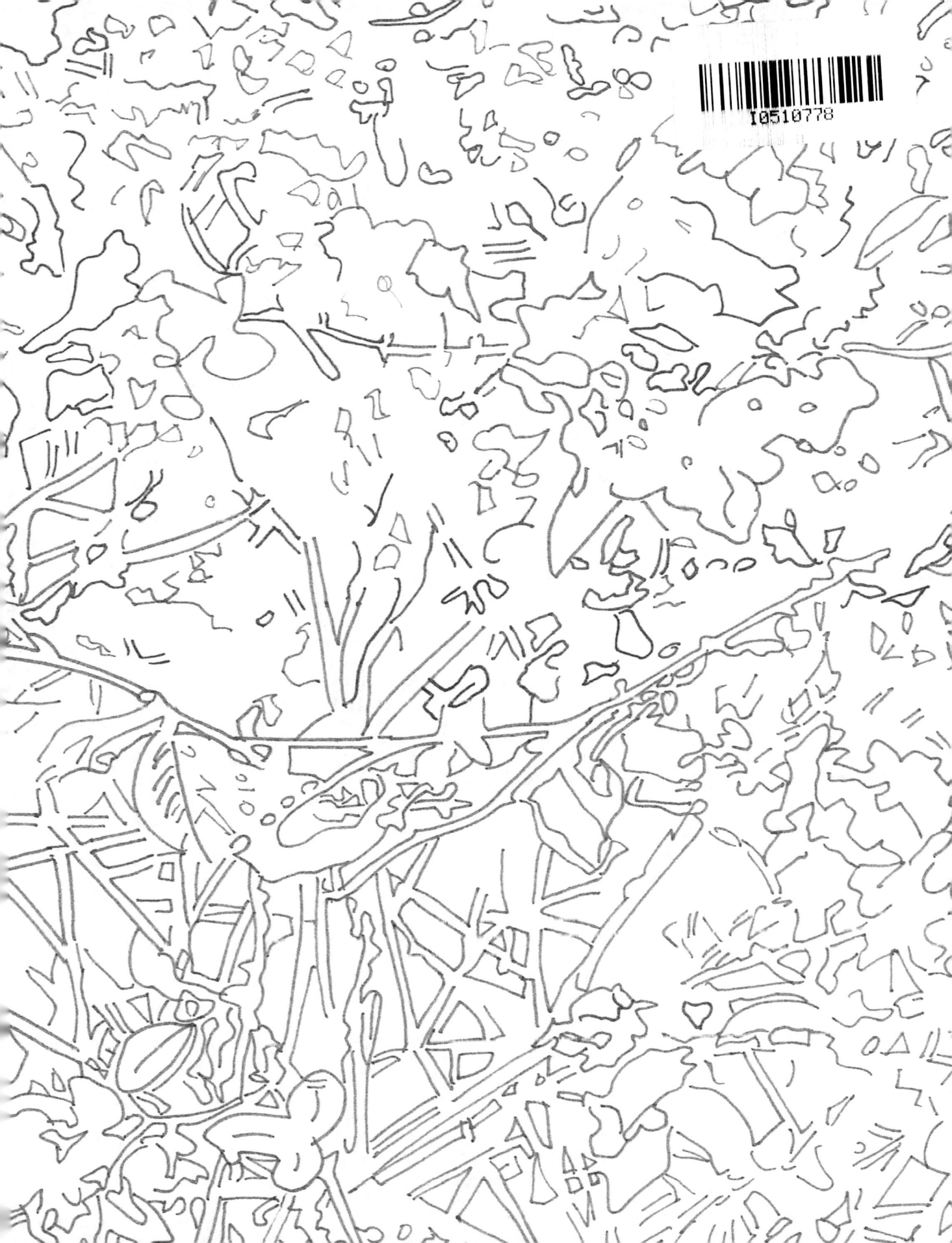

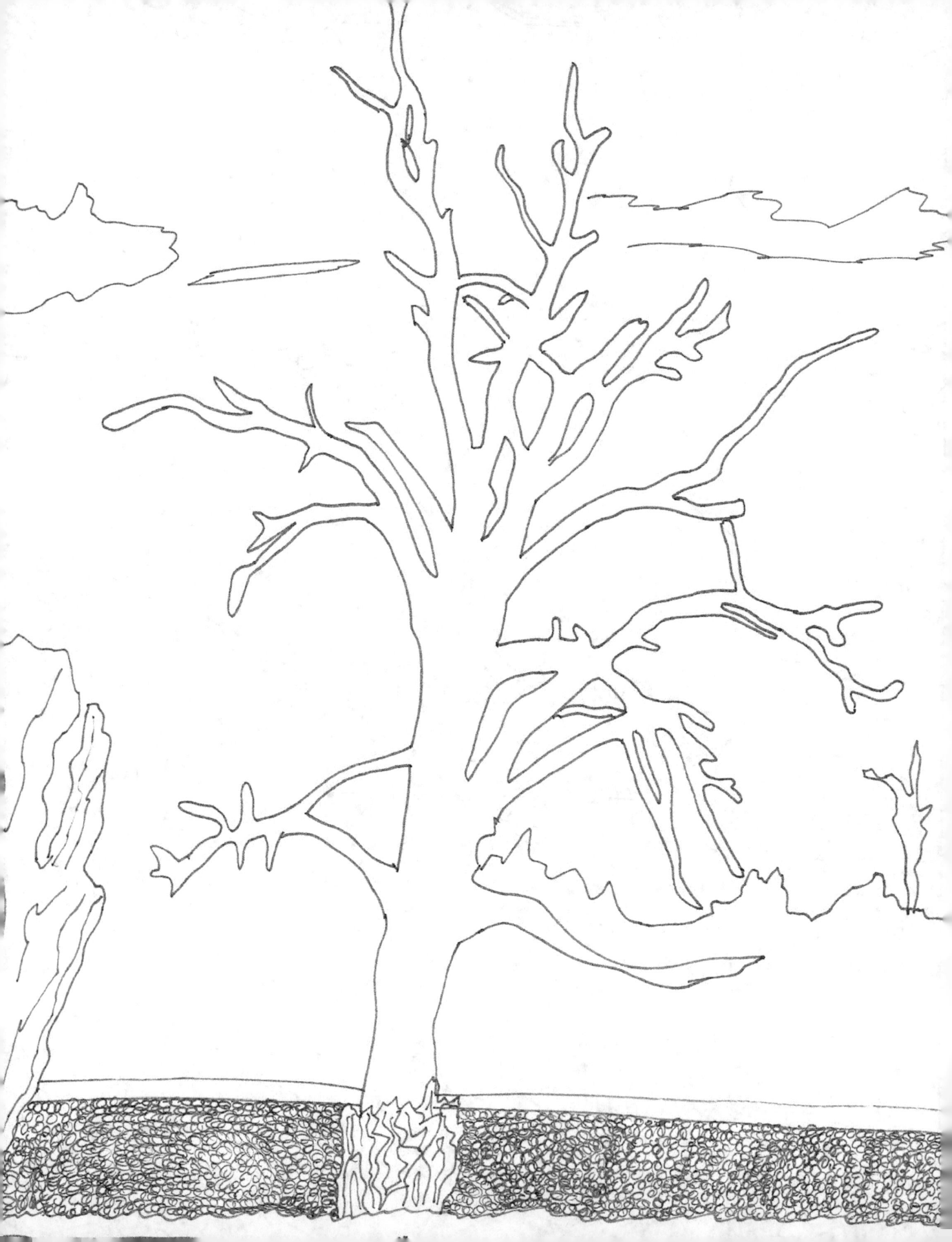

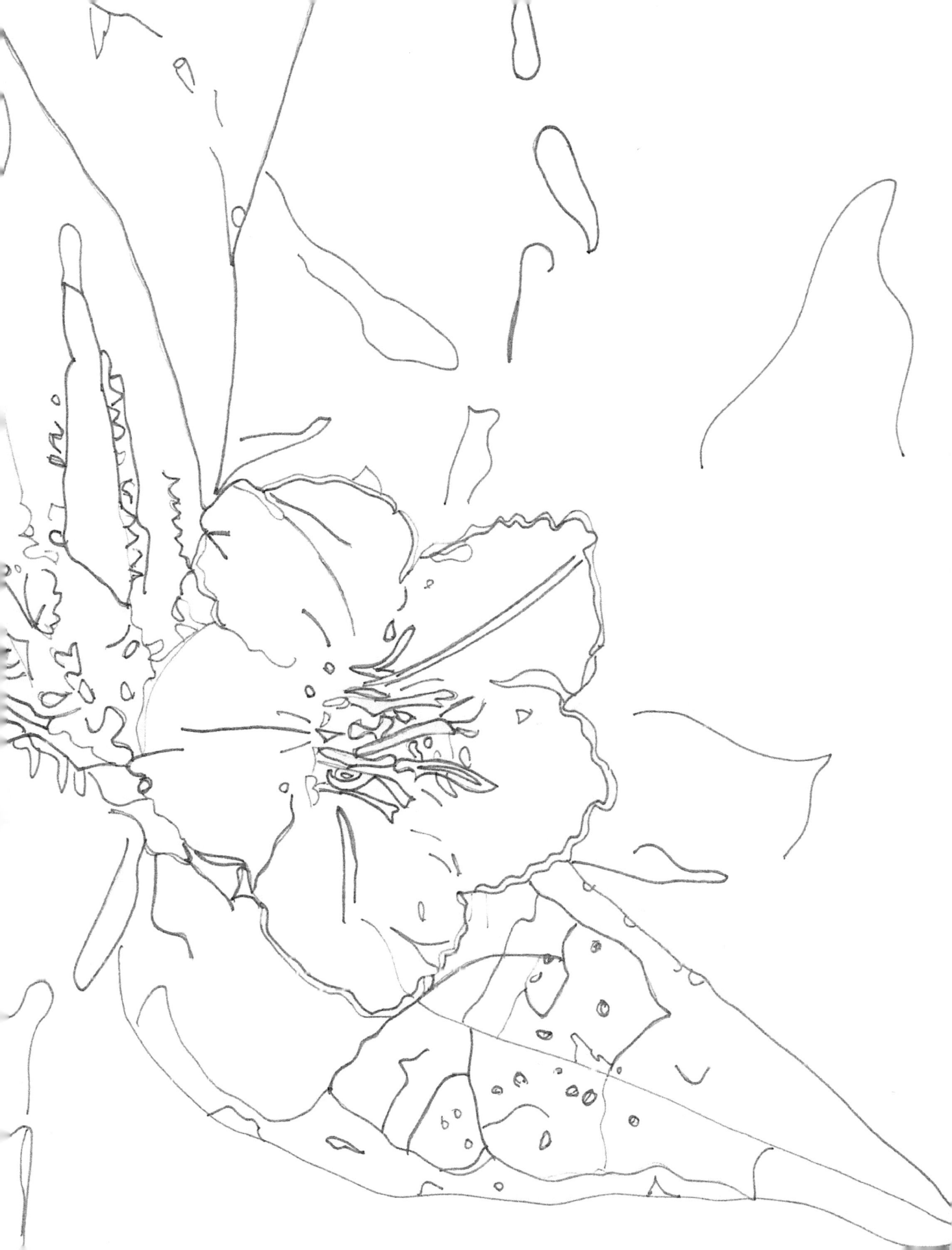

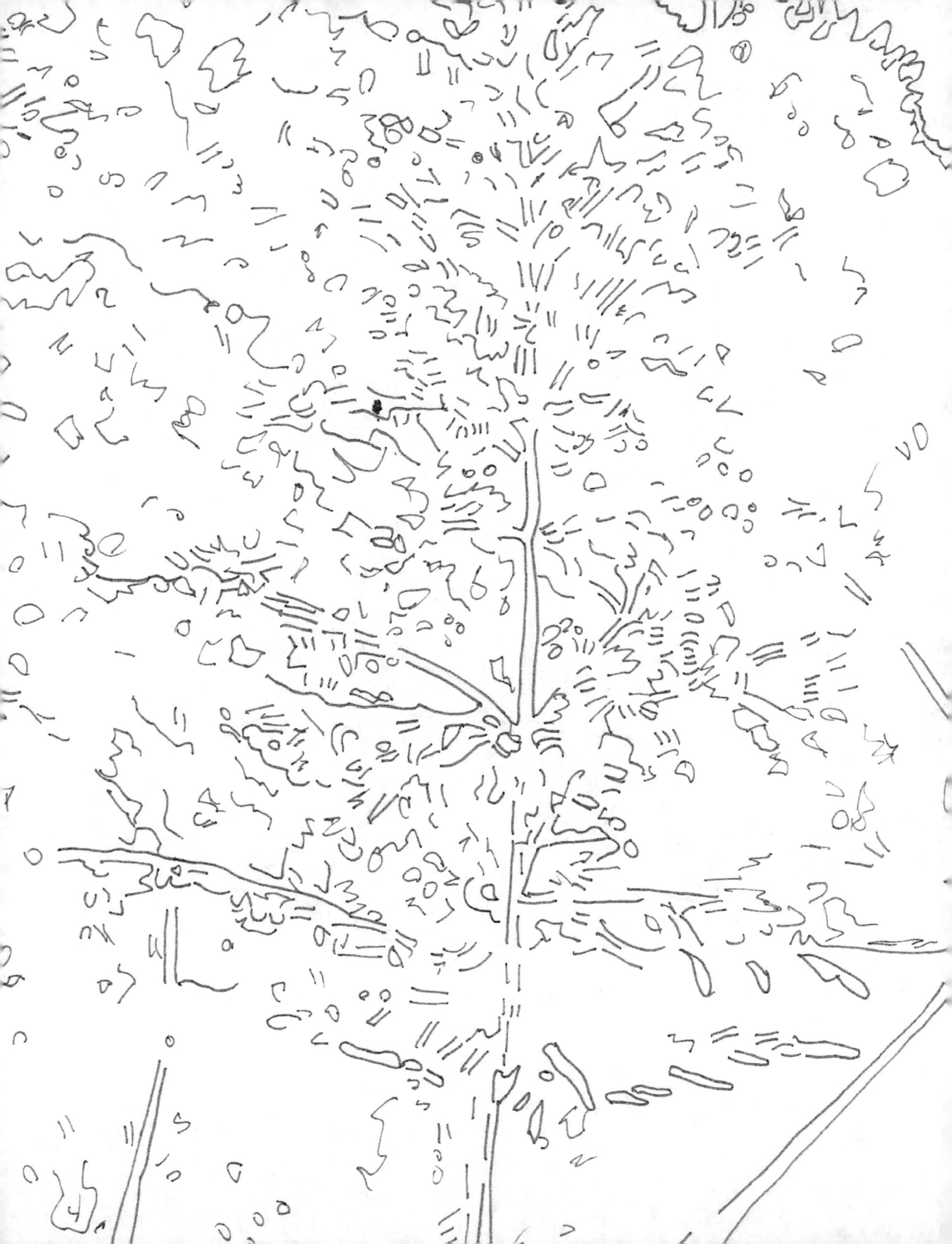

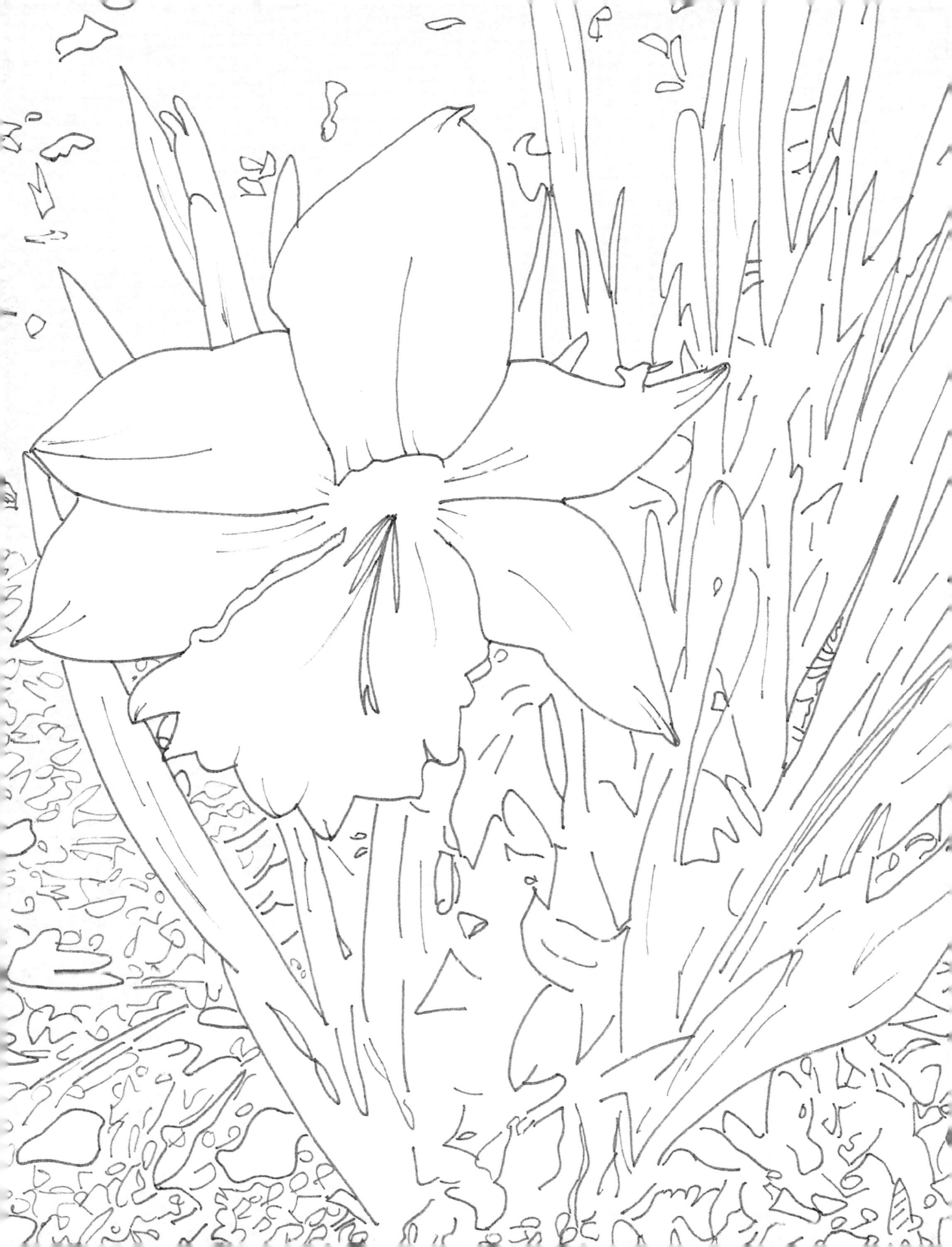

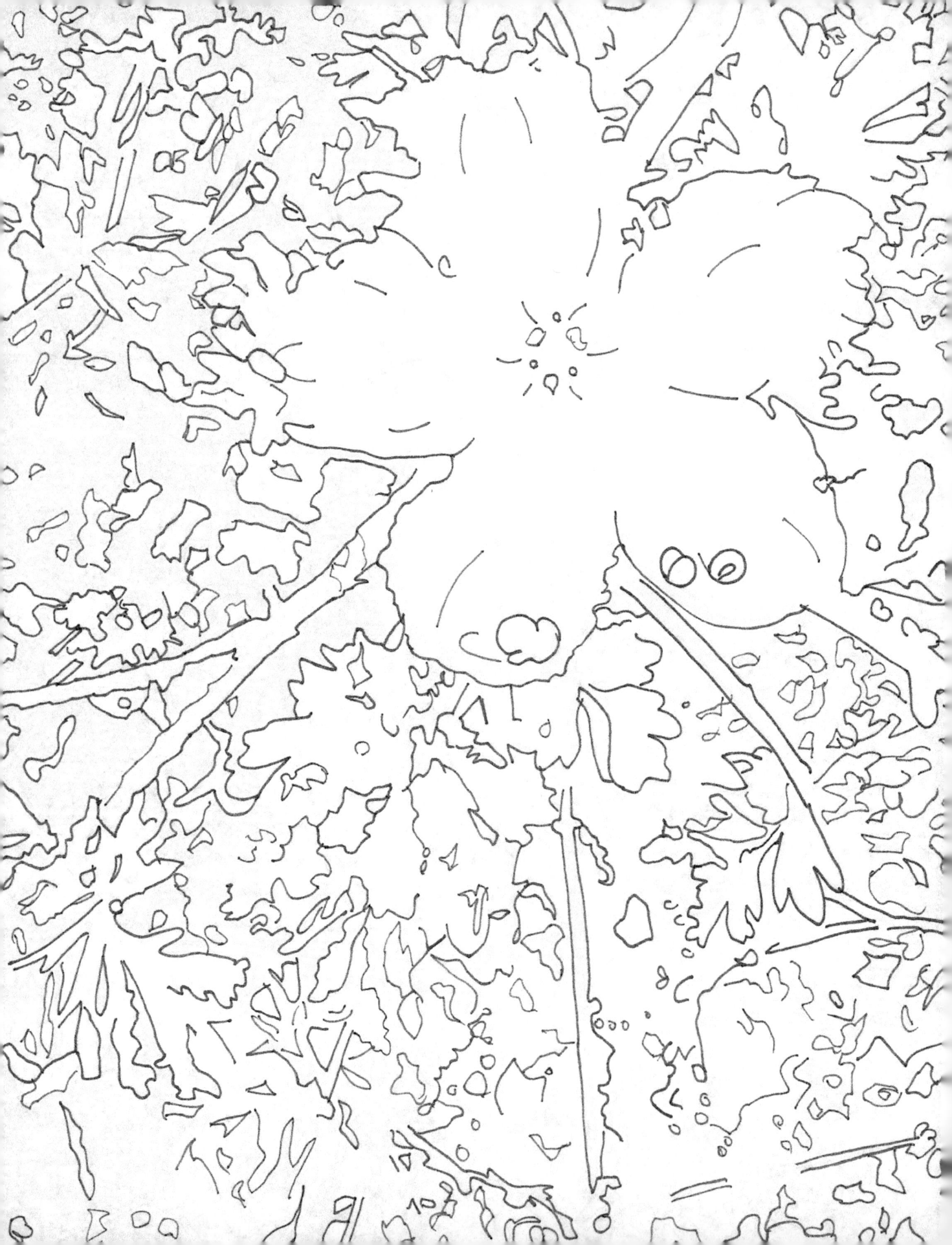

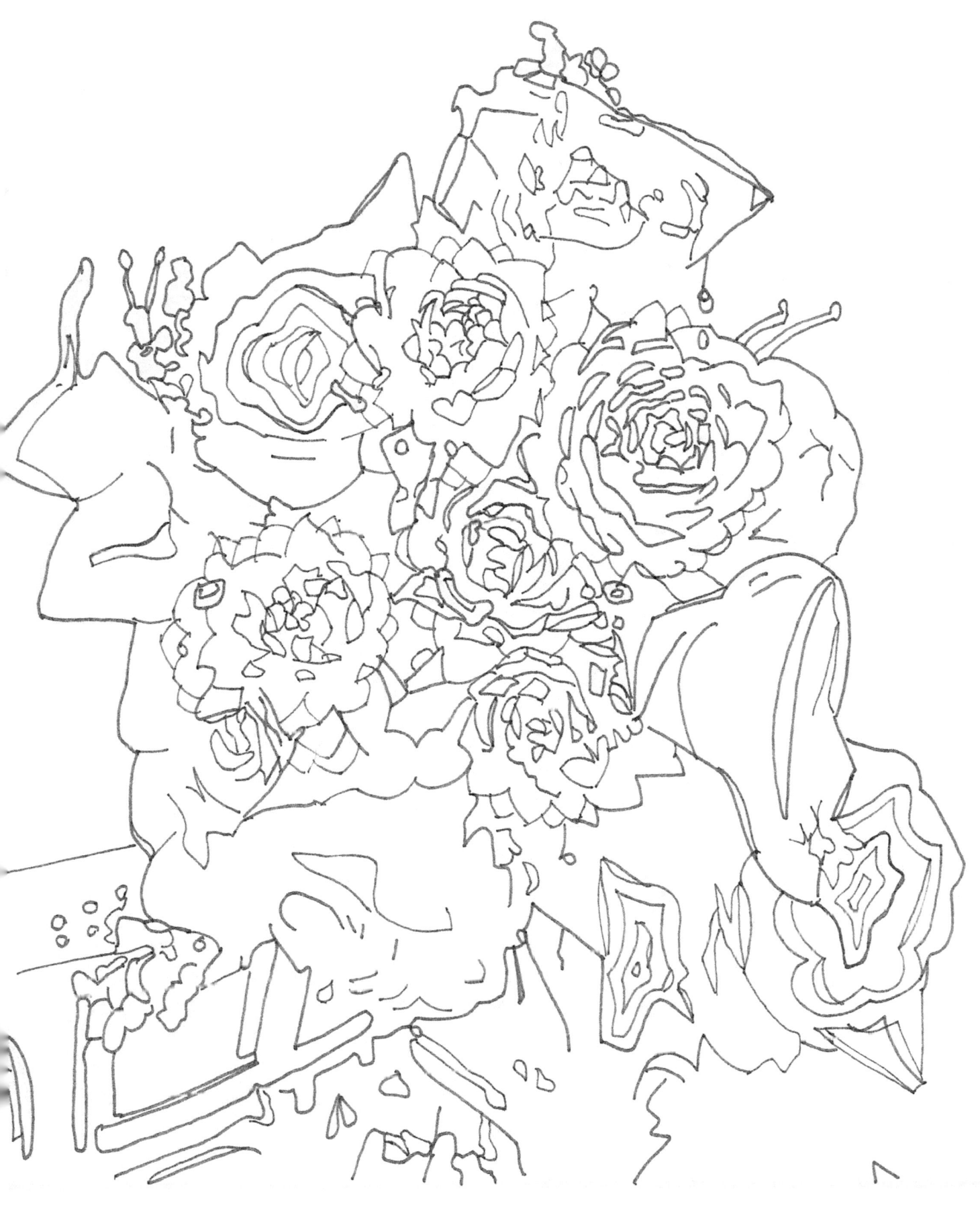

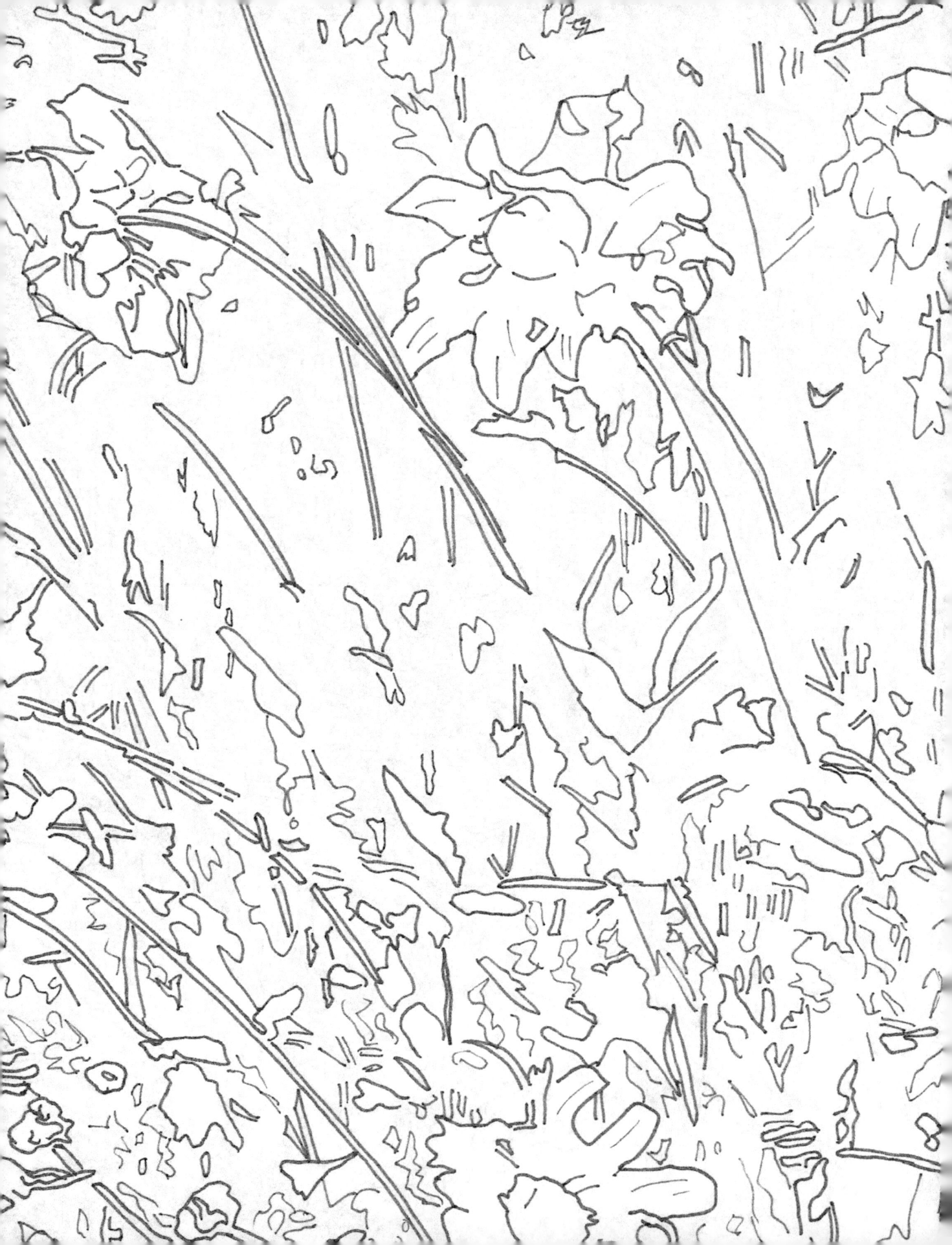

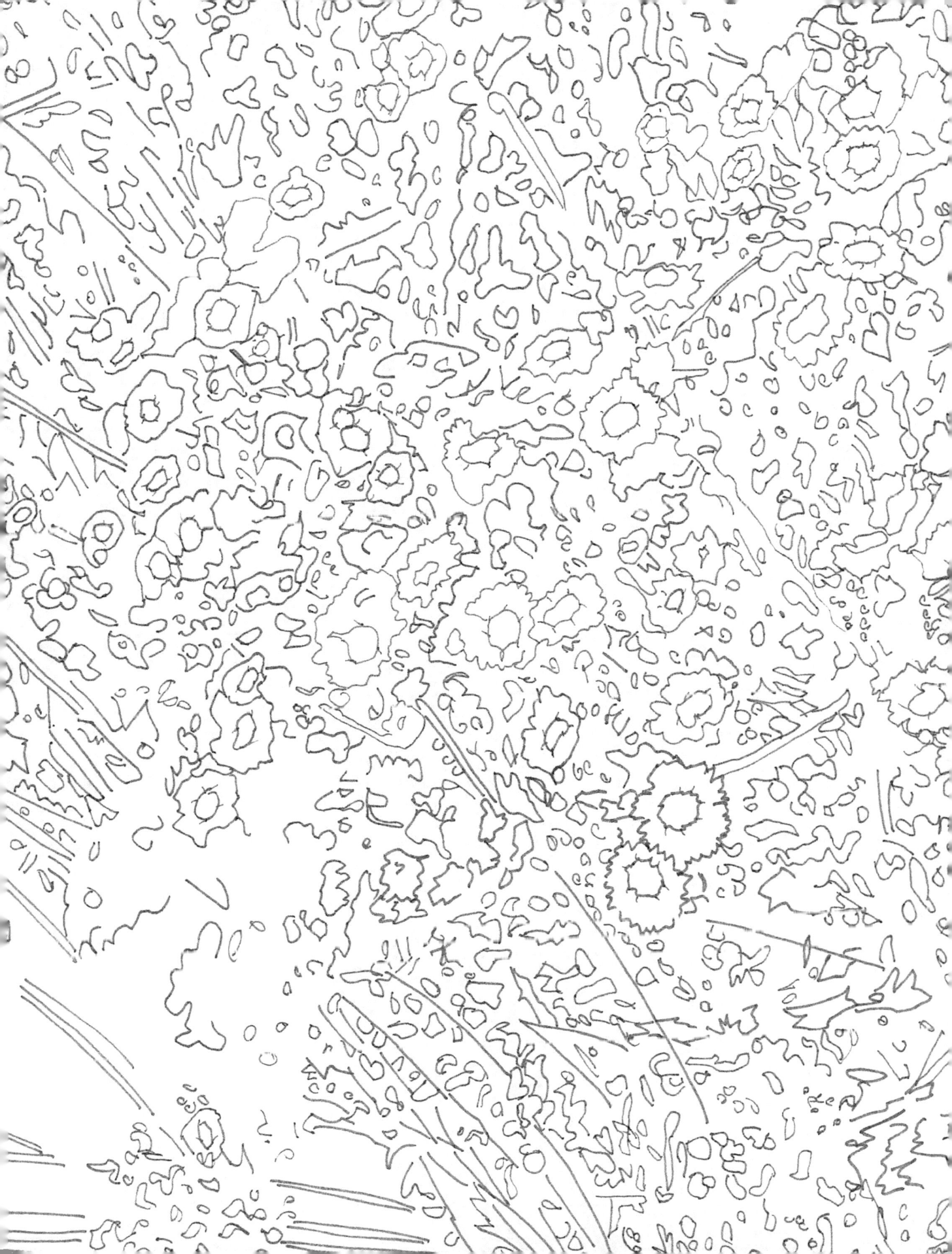

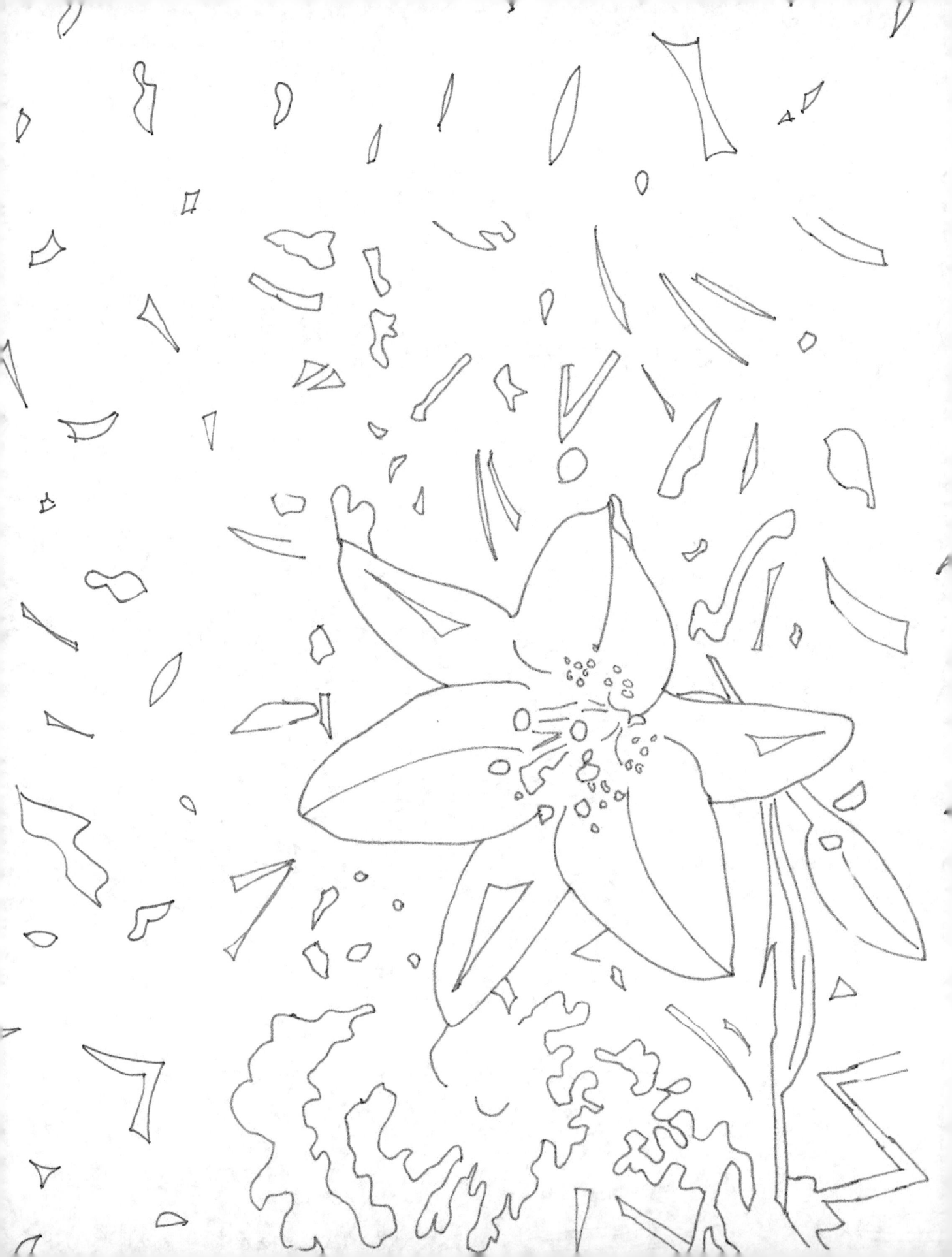

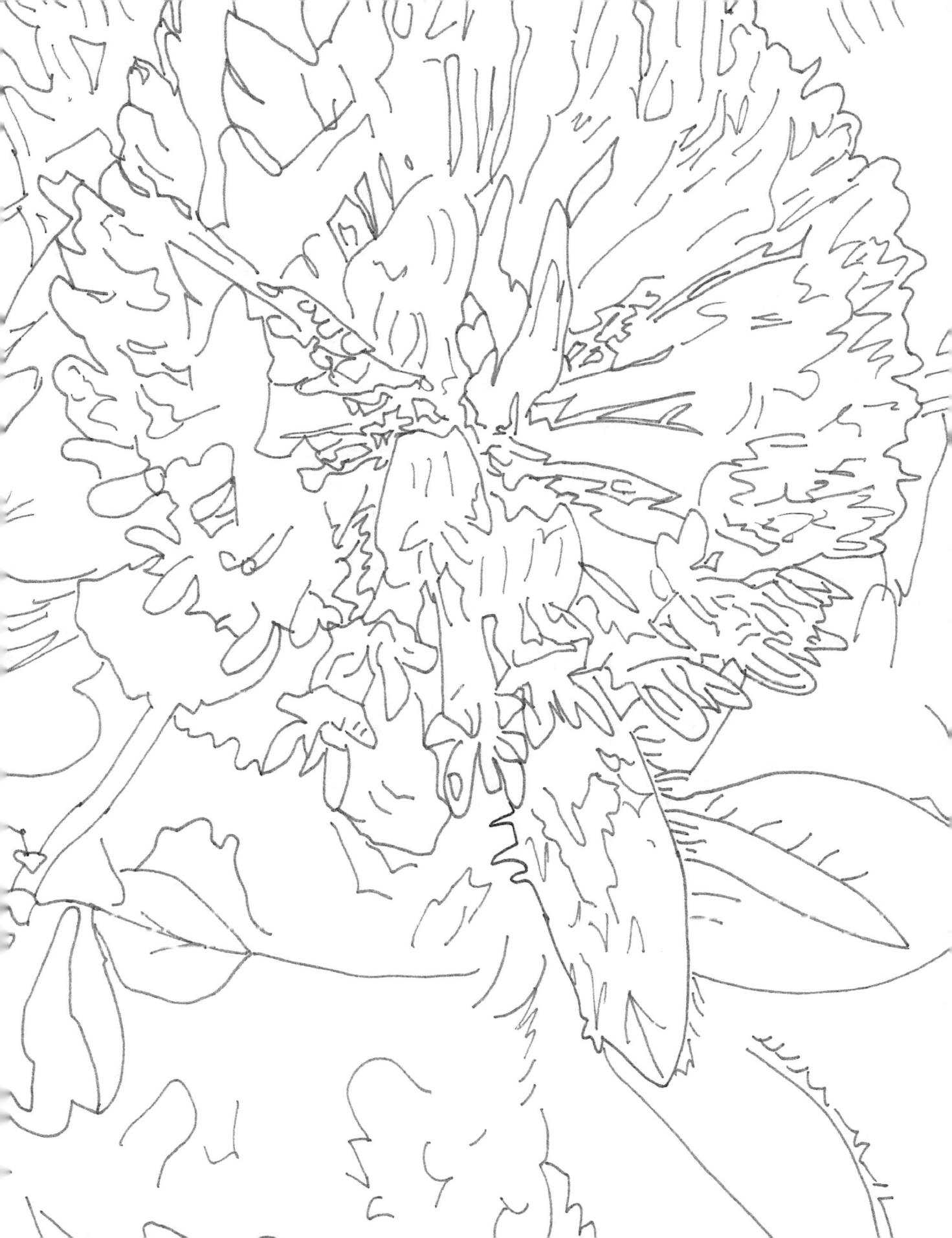

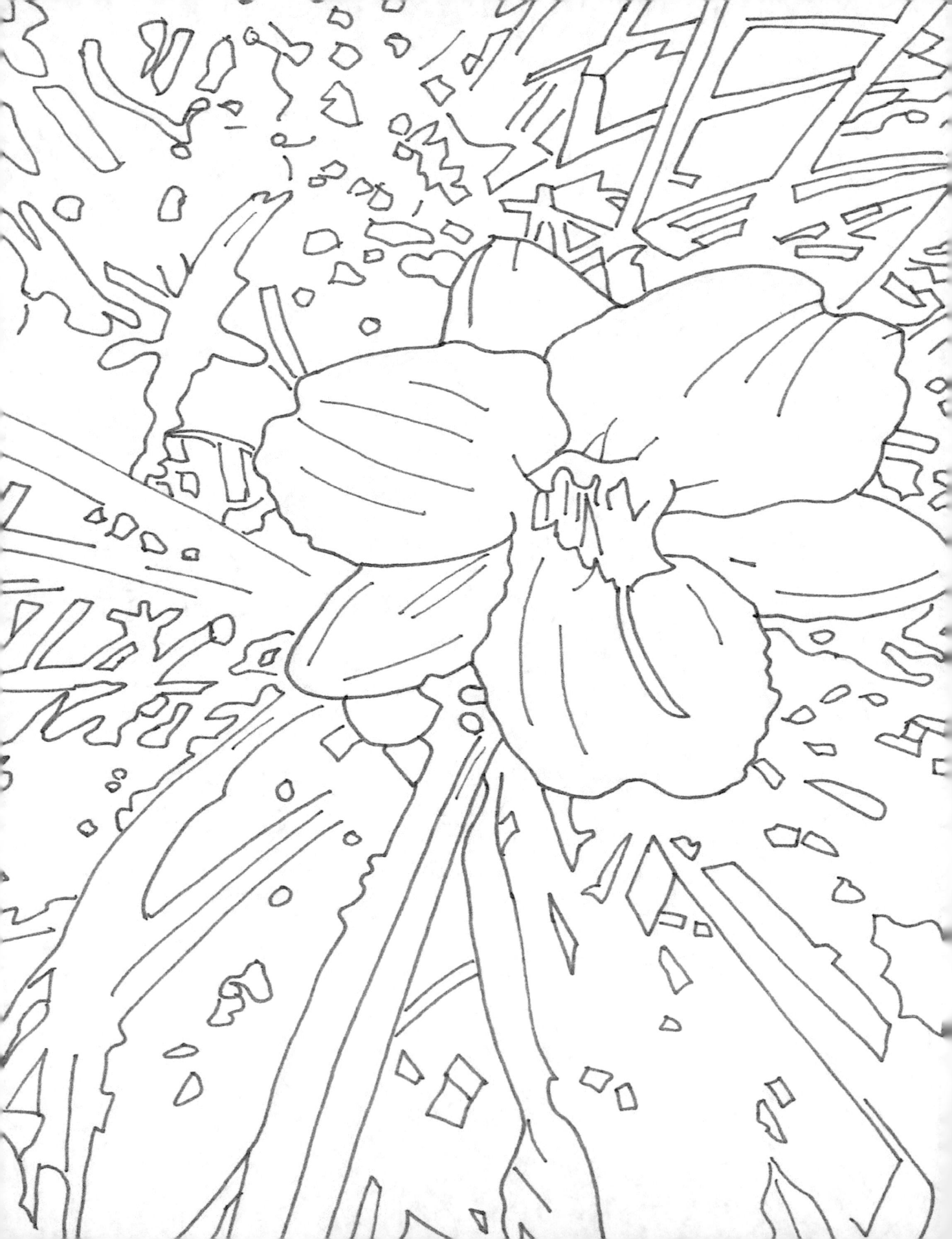

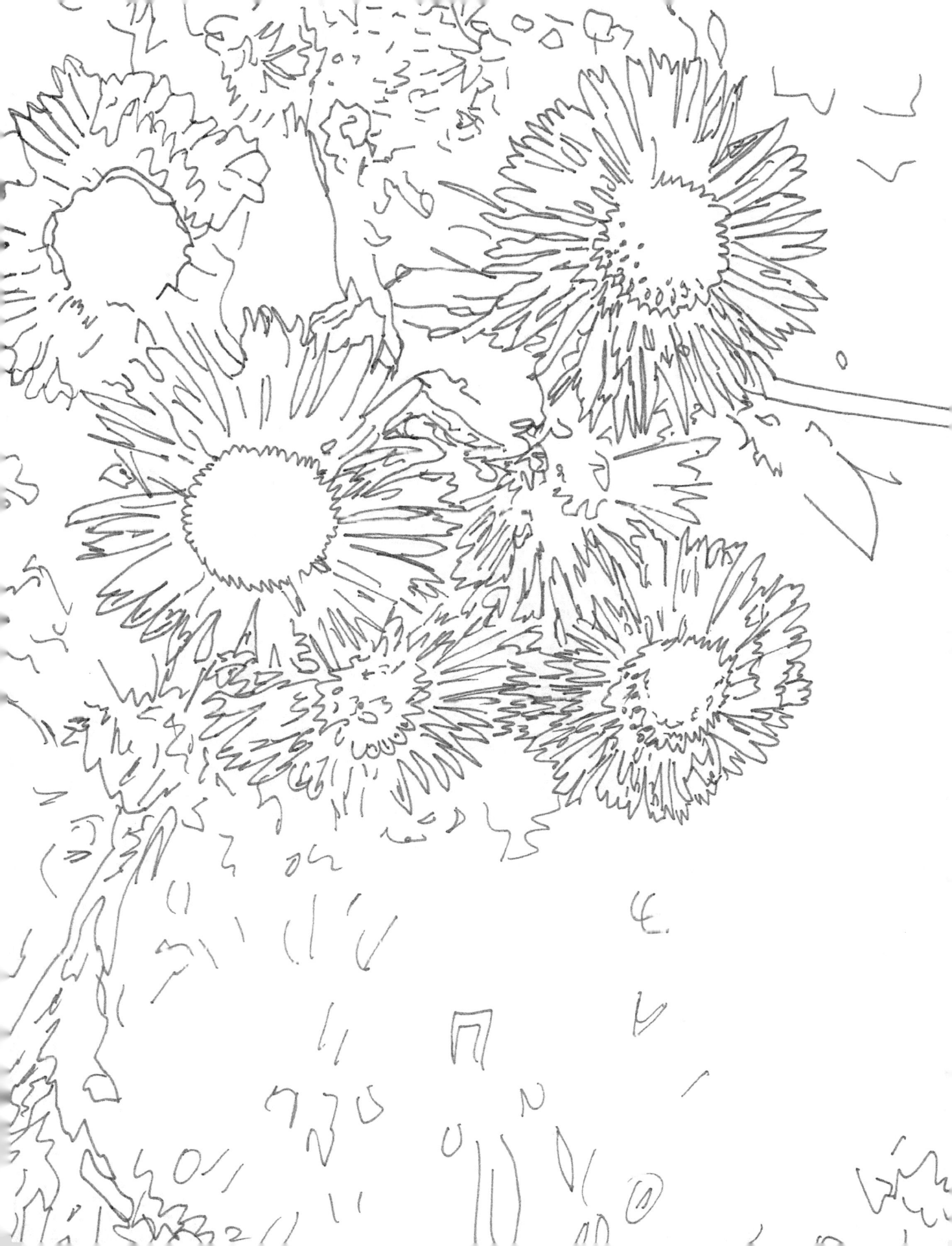

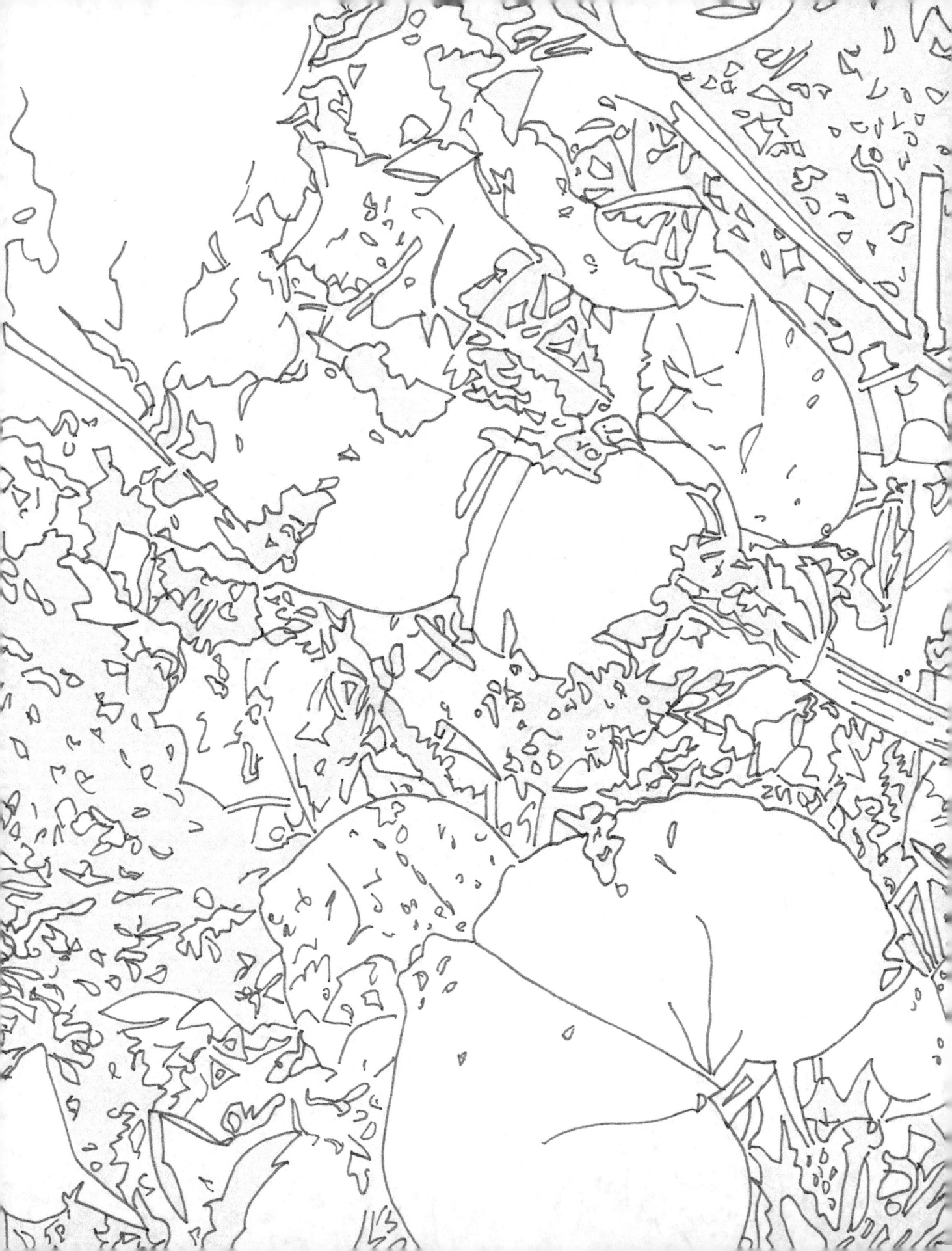

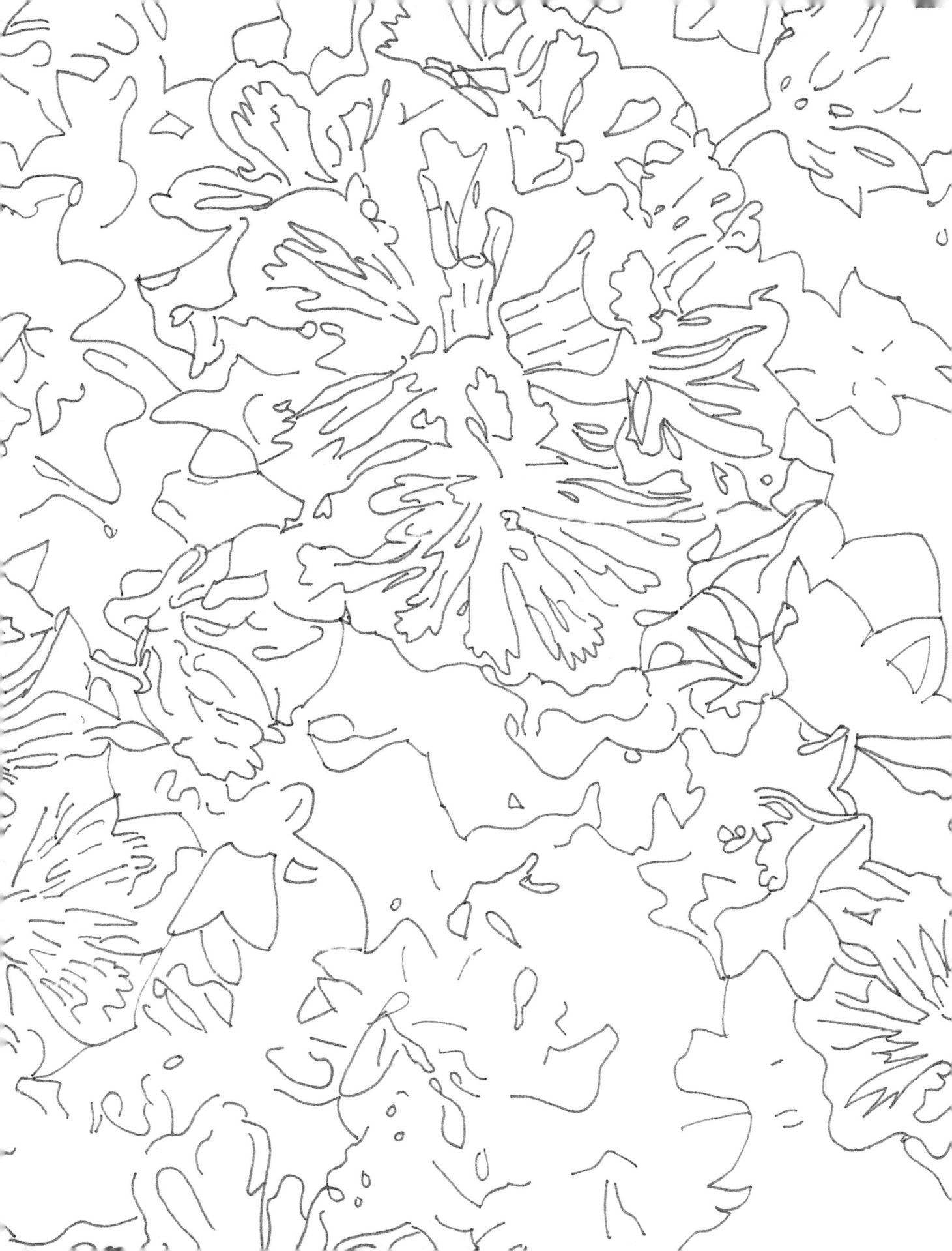

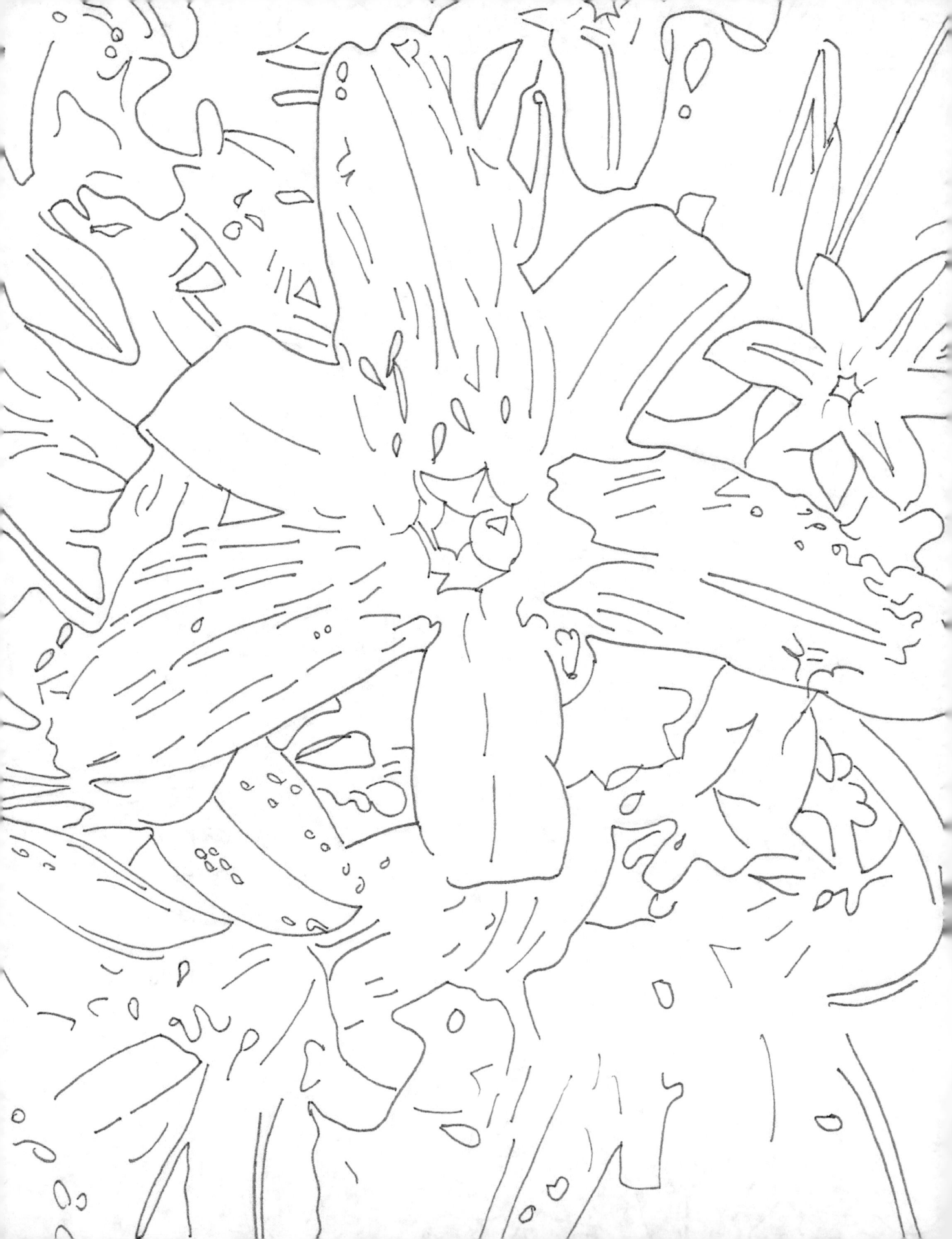

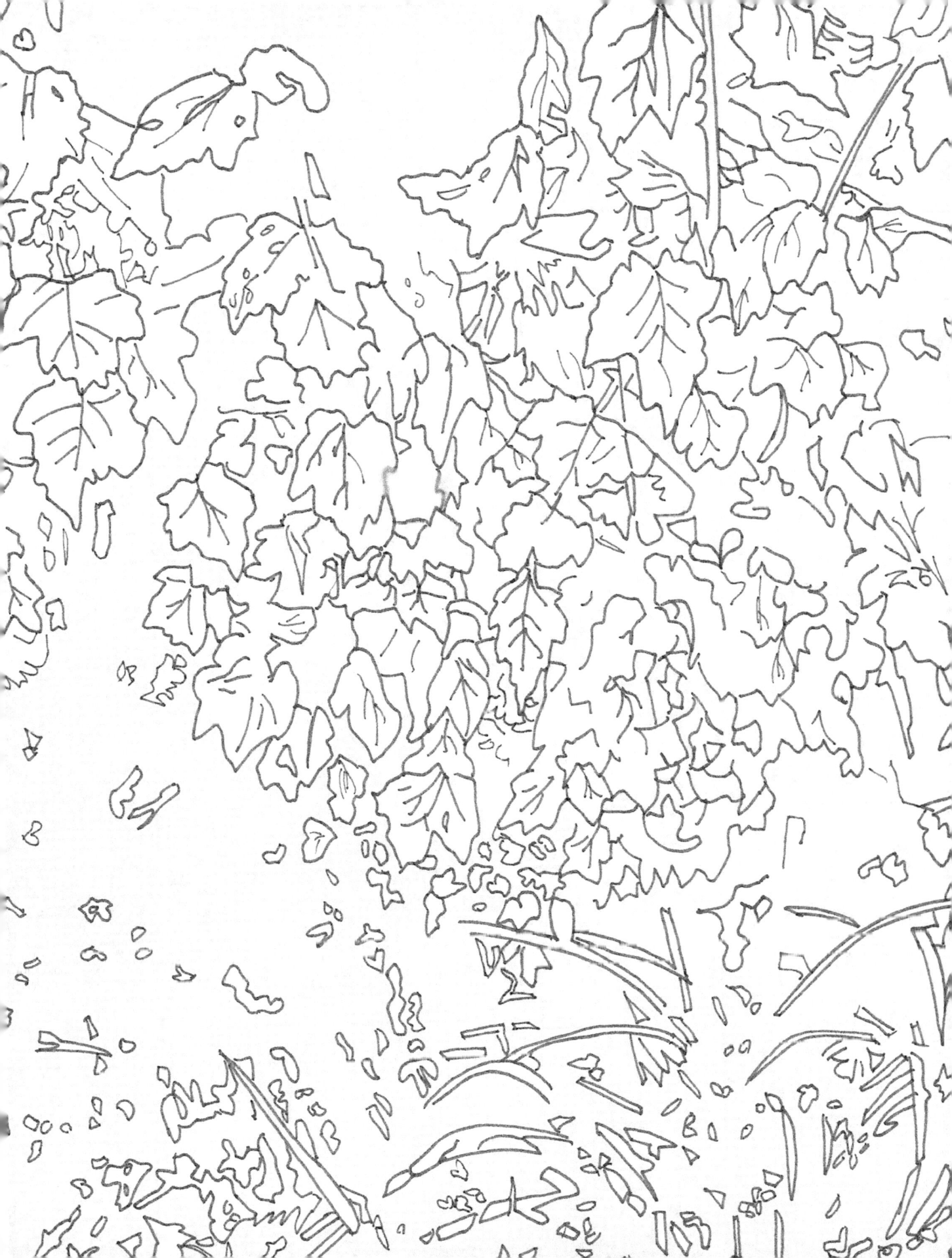

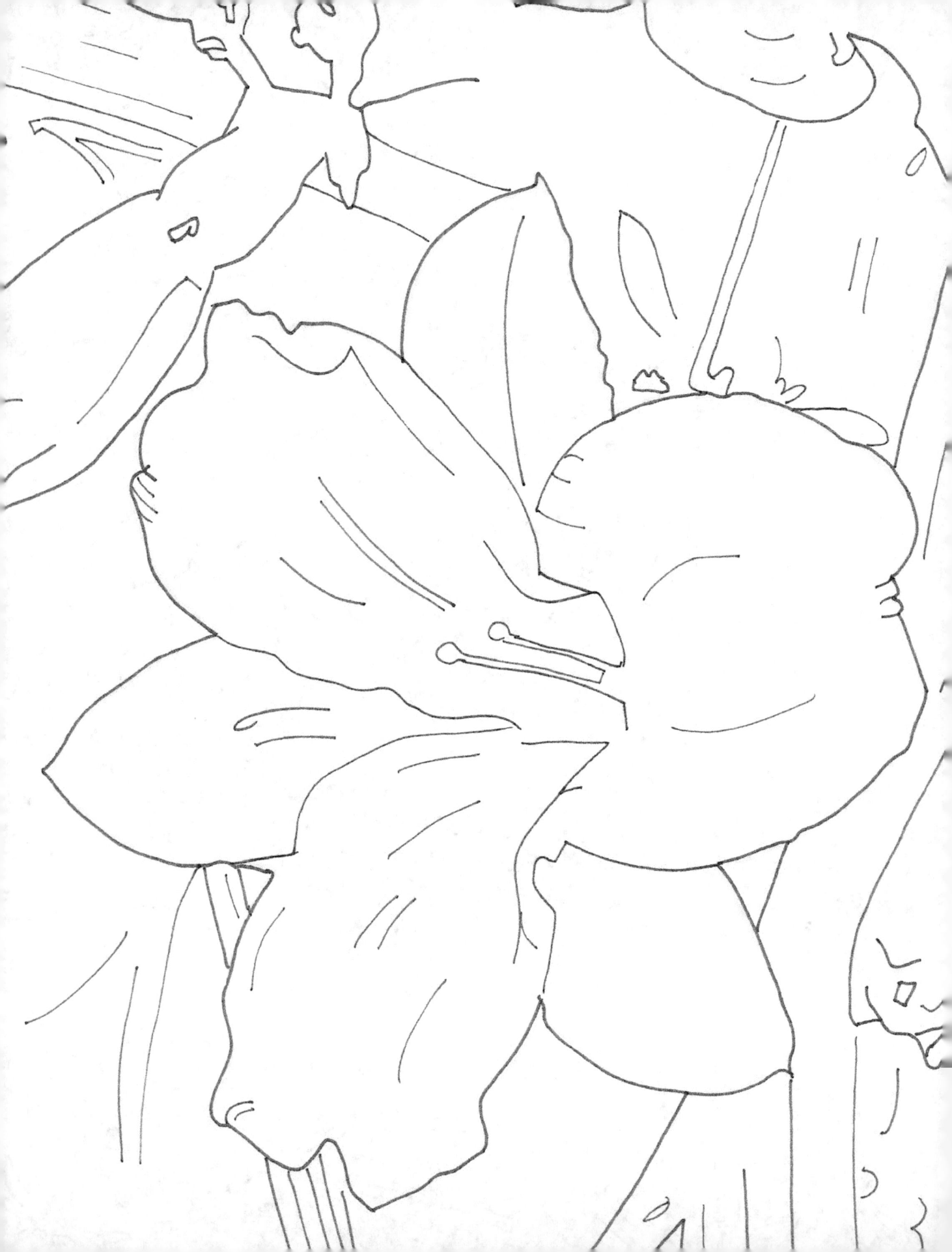

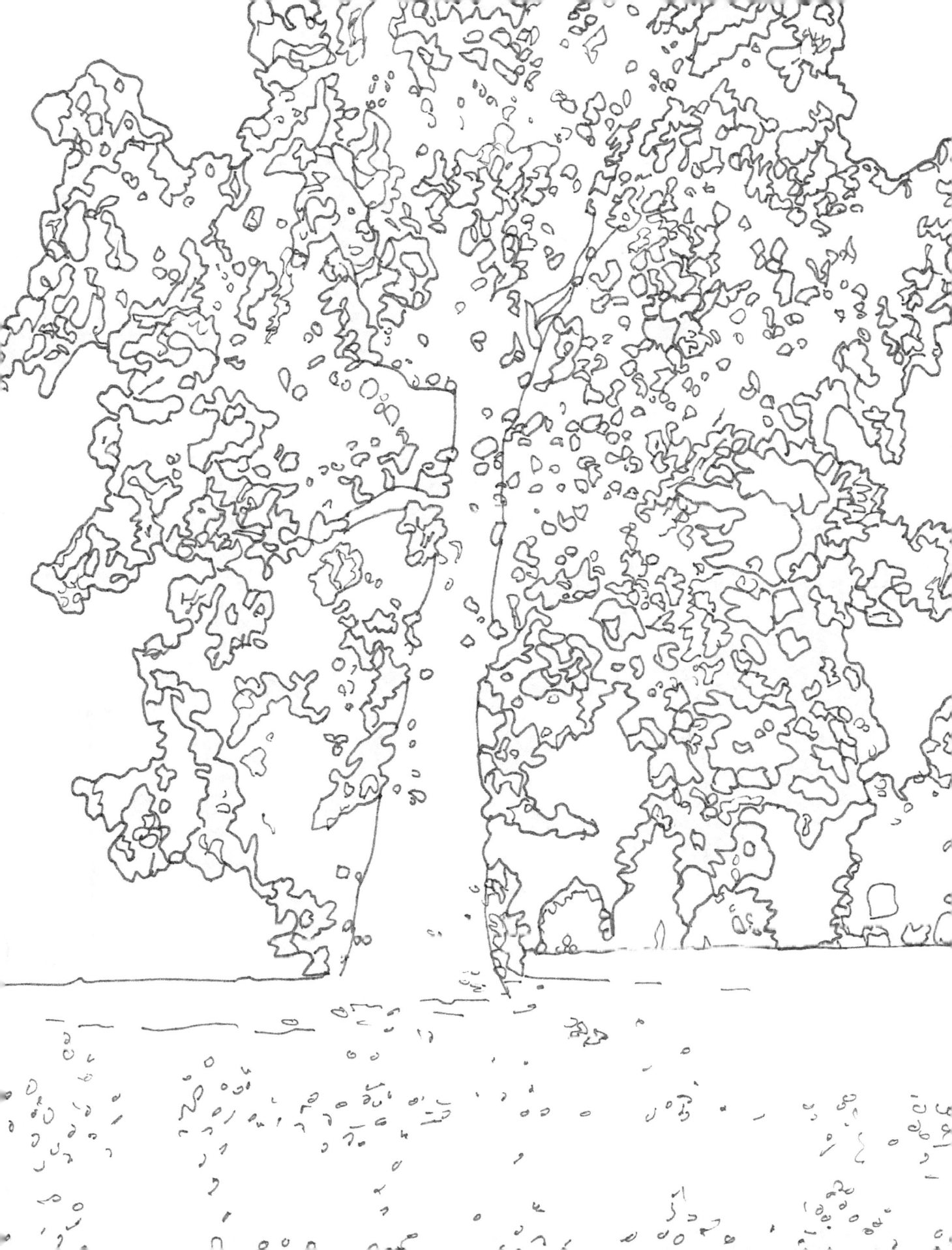

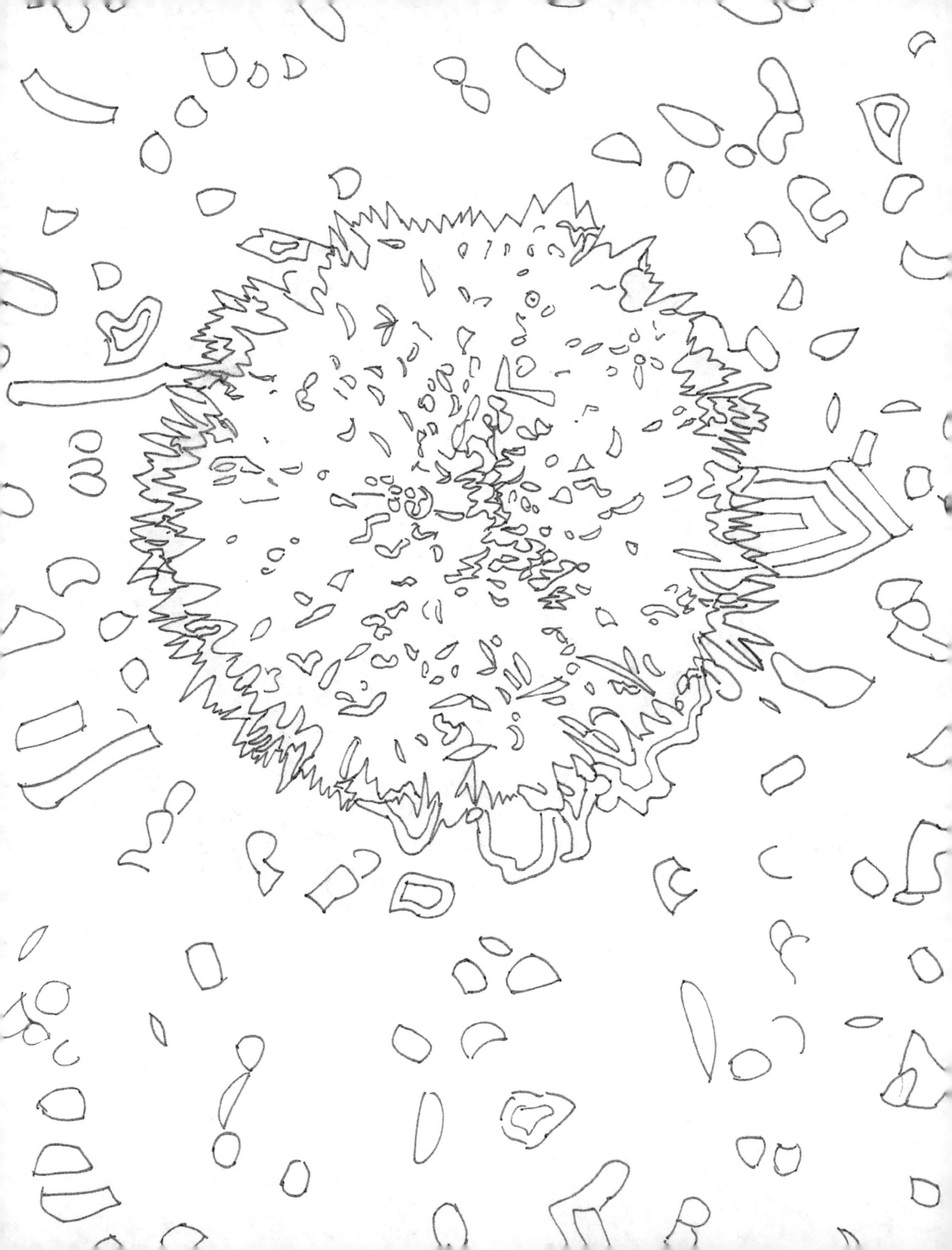

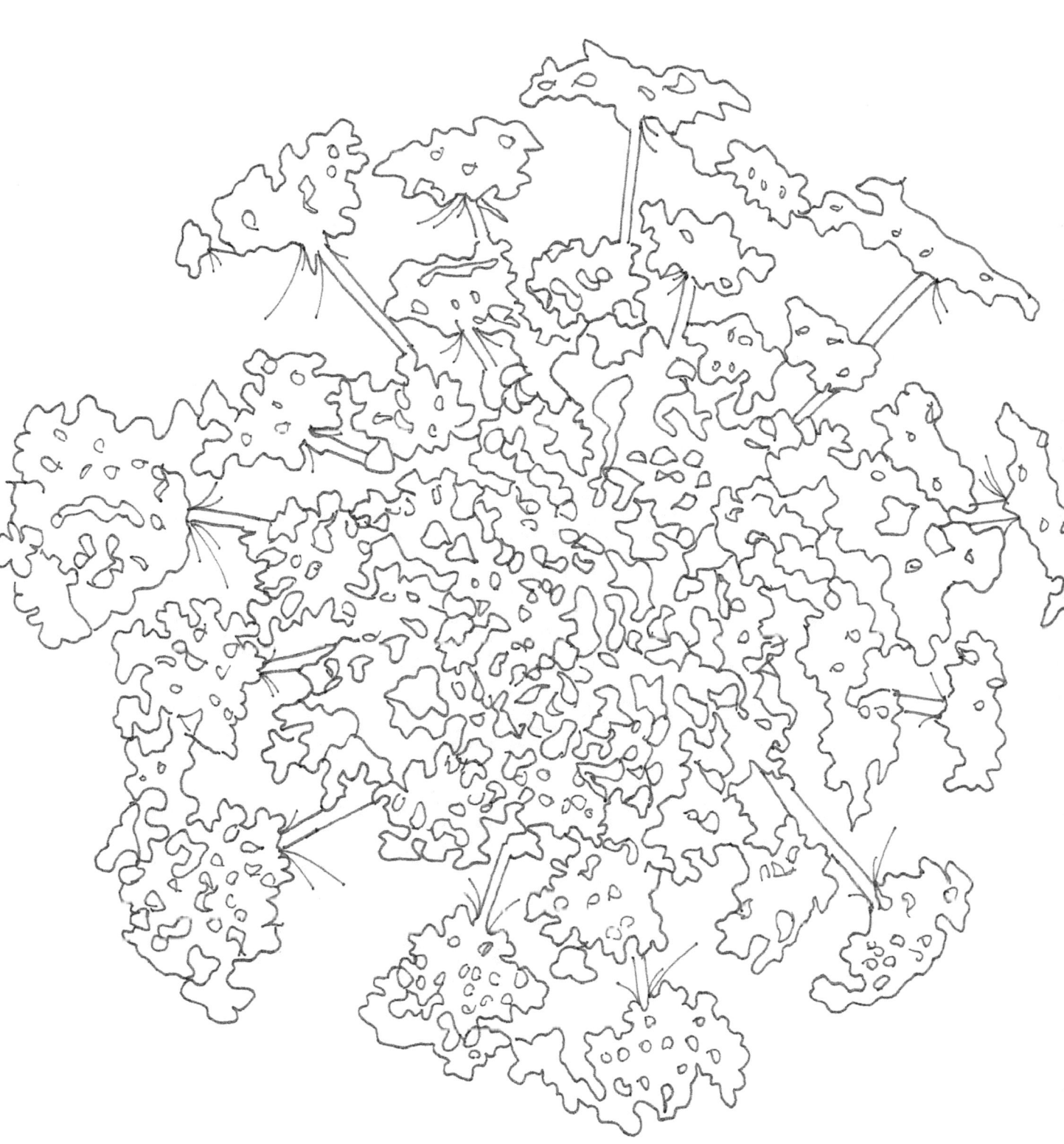

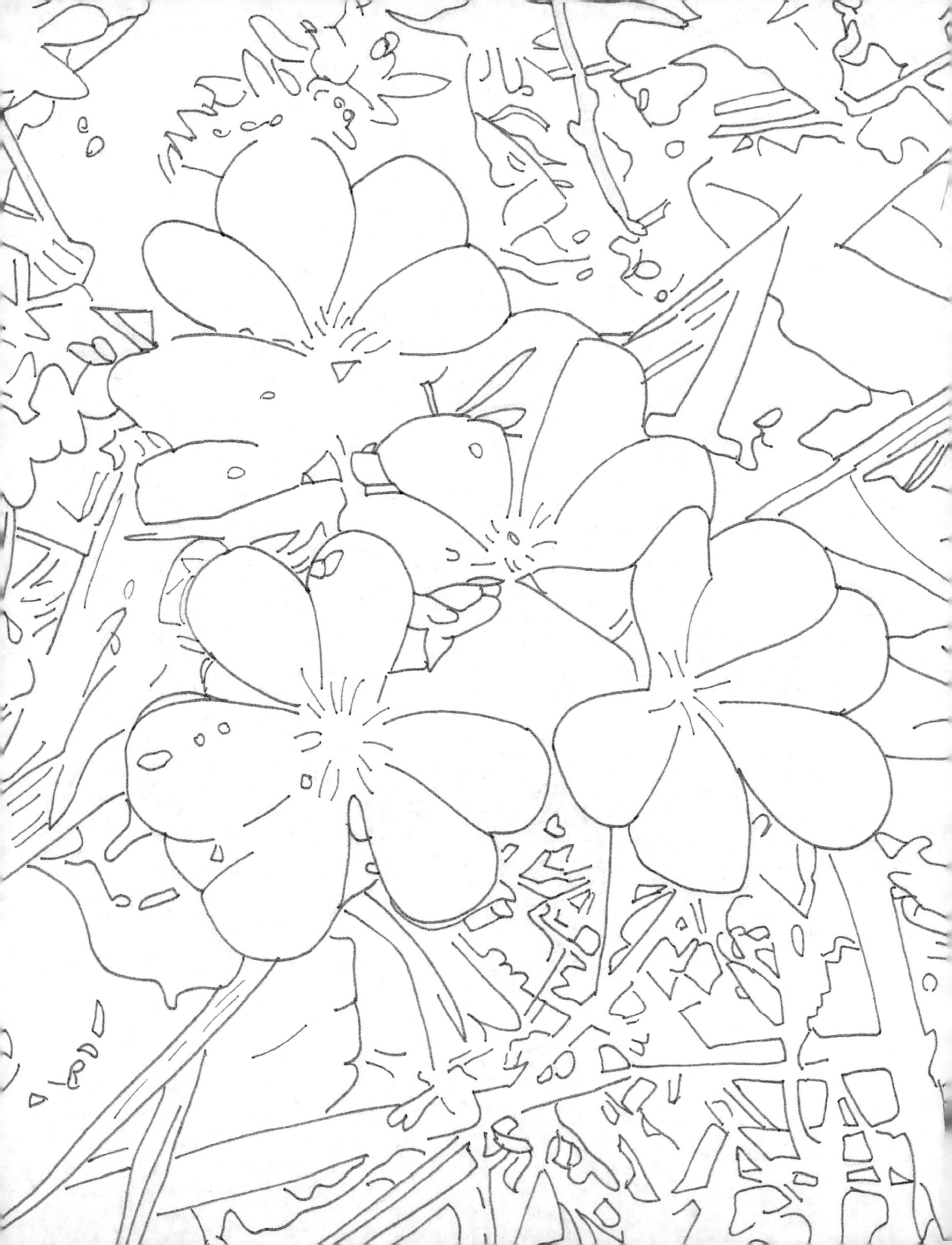

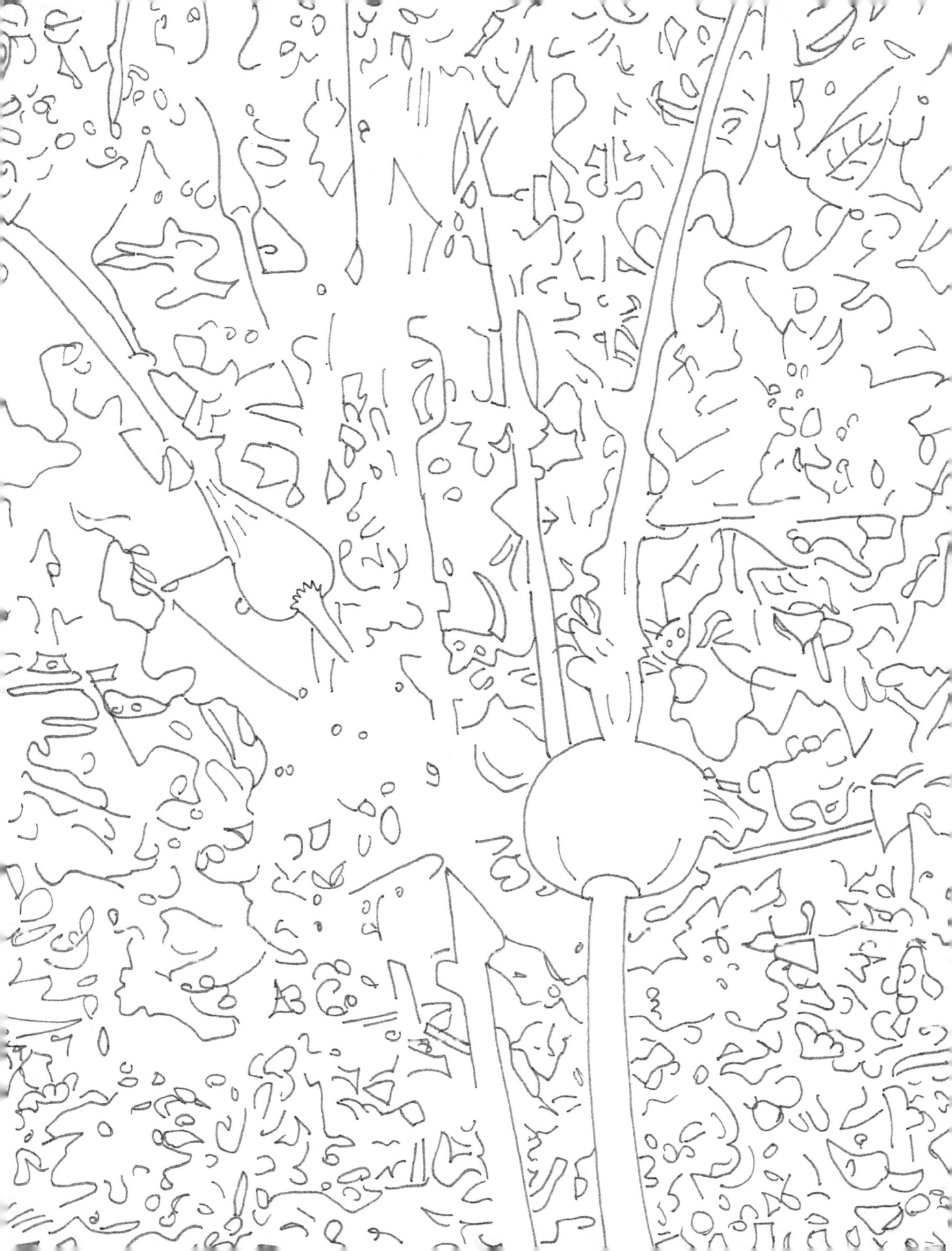

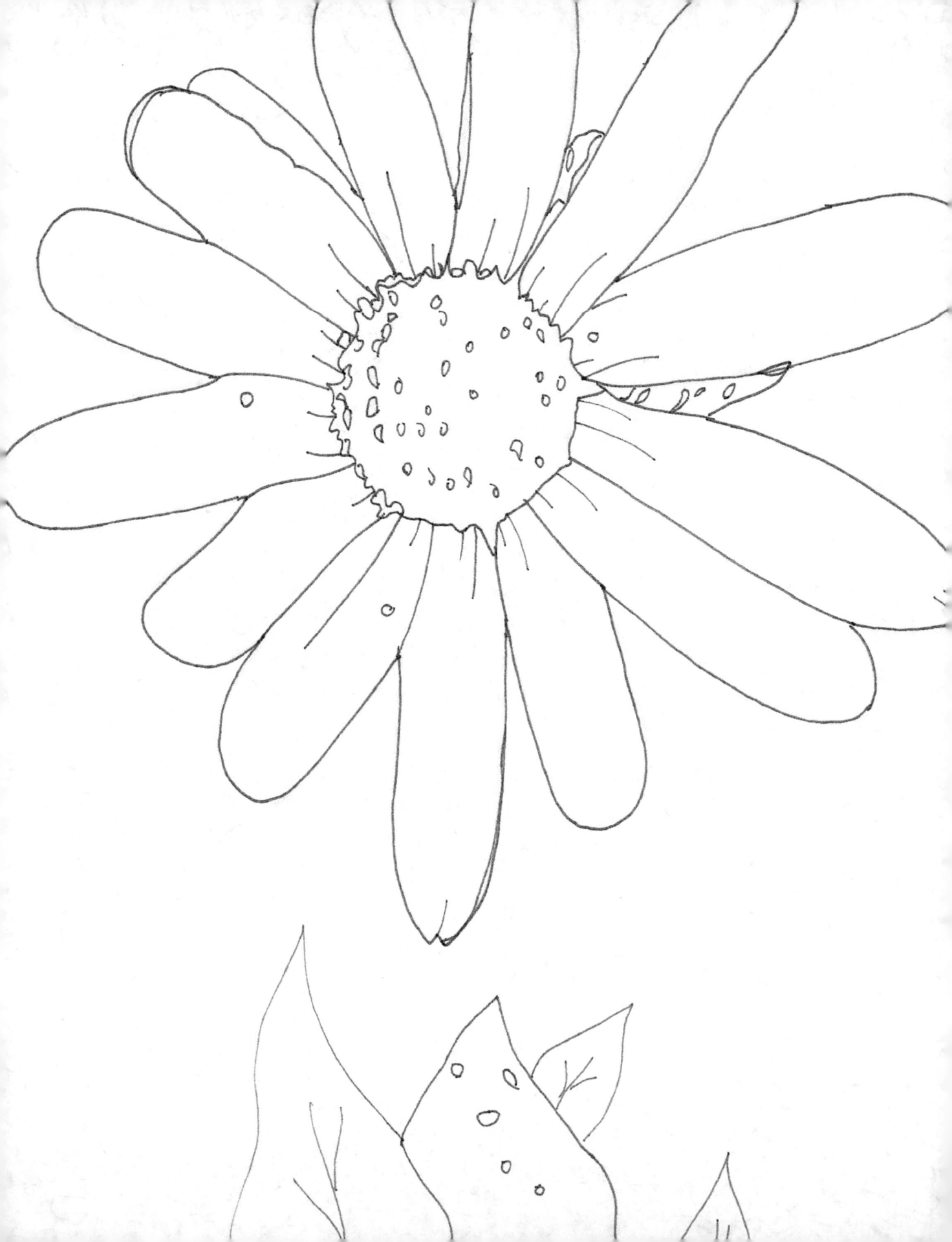

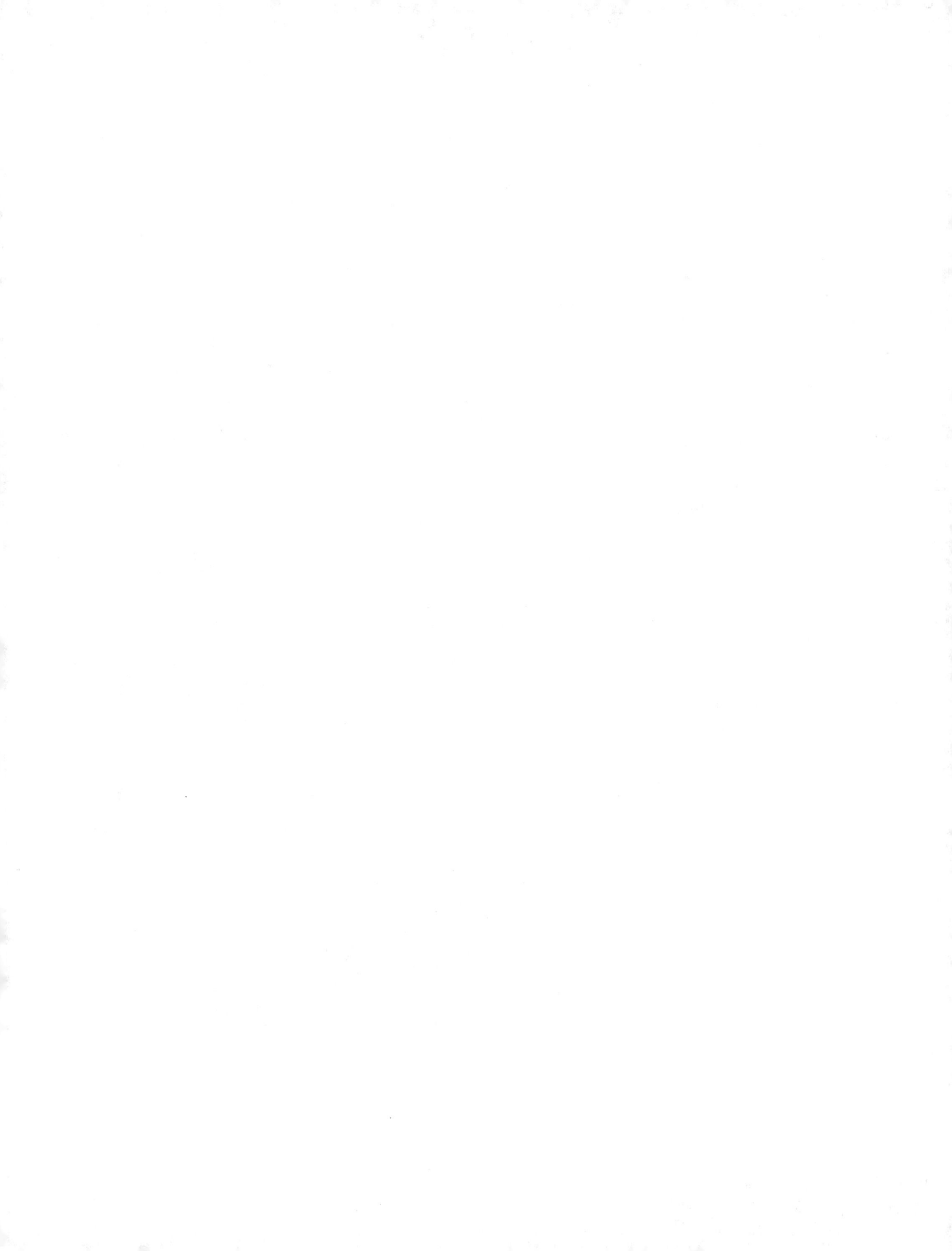

Ball lightning, the rapidly spinning electromagnetic field.

Natural ball lightning is a field of force which is round ball shaped and which is spinning on its axis very rapidly.

It is probably spinning at exactly the speed of light, which means it must be turning at a rate of about 200 Million to 2 billion turns per second, depending on its size. If all of it is turning at exactly the speed of light in the spinning motion, the inner parts of it must be doing many more turns per second than the outer parts of the ball. For example assuming every part of it moves at the same speed the outer fields of ball lightning might spin at 100 million turns a second, while the smaller inner areas of the sphere might spin at 4 billion turns per second. Obviously it would be interesting to make something which spins that quickly.

It is an electromagnetic field with a shape like a round ball spinning on its axis. It would only become visible when it has been given a lot of energy. So it might be more common than it seems, as weaker spinning fields of the same type might be transparent and invisible in almost every case, and so they would not be noticed.

The same type of spinning field should exist with a very wide range of different sizes and different energy levels. Sizes and energy level would not be connected, but should be completely separate variables.

Spinning fields which have a resemblance to it and are related to it, can probably exist in a whole spectrum of sizes all the way from hundreds of miles in diameter, to microscopic sizes. Just as light waves can have an enormously wide range of different wavelengths, from a wavelength of hundreds of miles to tiny wavelength.

Ball lightning is made from photons, but the photons of light manifest in a different structure, not as waves but as a round spinning field. While they are making the round ball they are not waves. I's amazing, I believe the photons of light or of radio waves can produce a structure of fields which is shaped as a round spinning ball.

I don't know what contracts the natural ball lightning into a round ball shape, but I understand a method of creating artificial ball lightning which would be very closely related to the natural thing. The at least approximately round ball shape in the artificial case is easy to understand.

Once you have made the artificial balls of lightning they would sometimes explode, especially they would explode if something metallic moves into them, and something absolutely identical to the natural thing should be created too in an explosion where they go bang and blow up.

An explosion of ball lightning could consist of the field which normally spins in small circles, suddenly flying out in straight lines. And then, after flying a fairly short distance in straight lines, some of the field could start spinning in small circles again. Which would form several secondary balls of lightning, instants after the first ball exploded.

What contracts the natural ball lightning into a round ball? I think its steady pointing magnetic field must have a lot to do with it, but I don't really understand how. Obviously if air is spinning you would expect the air pressure to be lower at the centre, but is there anything of plain pure electromagnetic fields that can be thought of as a lowered pressure? When light passes through a slit and is diffracted, it is thought that the light wave is made of many tiny wavelets which have a slight "pressure" on one another.

Whatever the explanations, my idea for artificial ball lightning should work.

Anything moving in a circle always has a centripetal acceleration pointing toward the centre of the circle, measured in meters per second per second, and described by the simple fraction $\frac{V^2}{R}$ Where V is the velocity in meters per second, and R is the radius in meters. Exactly the same acceleration is also written as $\omega^2 R$ Where omega is the angle velocity in radians per second, and R is the radius in meters. A radian is the angle where the radius traces an arc equal in length to the radius. When anything is spinning in a circle it only needs one force to keep it moving in the circle, and that is a centripetal force which always points toward the centre. Only one force pointing to the center, is necessary.

About flying outward, you use the word centrifugal force.

The word centrifugal seems to be used more often than the word centripetal?

One is obviously more aware of feeling centrifugal force when things are turning. But the centrifugal force which you feel pulling outward is not quite a real force, it is called an equal and opposite tendency to fly outwards, because everything wants to move in straight lines.

Also the law of conservation of angular momentum would have an effect on anything that turns in a circle, giving it more kinetic energy if a force contracts it and makes it shrink, and taking away kinetic energy if it expands. The law of conservation of angular momentum would affect ball lightning, as if a magnetic field were to contract it smaller its energy would increase.

When it is created by a lightning strike, the electromagnetic field which went to create the ball lightning was at the beginning a part of a radio wave. It was to begin with just a certain part of a radio wave, never a whole radio wave. An extremely strong radio wave had to be filtered so as to remove parts of it. A part of the wave had to be removed by a filtering effect in the atmosphere in the natural conditions, or else the ball lightning would never have formed.

Further down I am going to go into the complete details of how the radio wave should be filtered.

I have read that Ball lightning is able to drift through glass windows, or plastic windows, and to carry on floating through the air on the other side, according to some people who say they saw it entering an aircraft through the glass of a window.

It apparently entered the cabin of an aircraft through a closed window and then floated in the air.

Someone seated in the airplane, as a witness said it floated before them and looked like microwave energy spinning, just after it floated in through the closed window.

And I have read people have seen it entering a house through a closed glass window.
Which shows that it must be purely a field of force, as matter is stopped by anything solid like a glass window.
 I have read that people who have seen it often said they think it must be related to microwave energy, and that it looks as if it is obviously spinning. And someone said he saw it floated calmly through the brick walls of a house, and emerged on the other side of the brick wall.

I believe the witnesses who said it floats through glass, and through plastic and through bricks, told the truth. And this means to me that the natural ball lightning could not have in its structure any electrical currents.
The natural ball lightning cannot have fire or gas plasma or any sort of burning mineral as a necessary part of its structure. Well there could be some of those things in it sometimes, but never as a necessary part of it. When it floats through a closed window, it is pure electromagnetic field, nothing else.

It has to be purely a field of force, able to exist without electric currents, able to float through glass and plastic windows as a field of force. This proves that it cannot have electric currents in its necessary structure since electric currents would have been stopped. Apparently a witness said it entered his house through a brick wall. So it never depends on electric currents, but, when it generates electric currents, that would be a form of friction which would wear out its energy and decrease its lifetime.

I think it is made from photons, but whether the photons are exactly the same particle as photons of ordinary light is not quite certain. They probably are the same or a similar kind, but they are doing something different.

I read that some witness said ball lightning flew into a barrel of cold water and the water became hot. I think this story gave the impression that it lasted for at least a few seconds under the water, and the water became hot.
Though it can store a lot of energy, it stores energy purely as an electromagnetic field which probably moves at exactly the speed of light in the form of spinning. But, can it possibly slow down over time? Or would it vanish immediately if its spinning ever started to slow down? It is plausible that the ball lightning had to move at exactly the speed of light in spinning motion?

 Like in a radio wave the electric field and the magnetic field of the ball lightning must be moving at exactly the speed of light, and because of that speed they would be considered to induce one another.
If the two fields induce each other, that is a form of self-perpetuating which is thought to work in a radio wave to give the radio wave the ability to move through space for any distance, any length of

time.

And like the radio waves, ball lightning could keep on spinning for ever, except that friction of several kinds in the air uses up its energy gradually and after a few minutes it's gone.

I think the two fields must be at right angles to each other and also at right angles to their direction of motion as they spin at the speed of light.

One of the reasons why I do assume that the fields in the ball lightning move at exactly the speed of light, is because I have read that at lower speeds you need to have electric charges to create an electric field. At the speed of light you do not need any form of electric charge. A radio wave goes forever through a vacuum where there might be no electric charges.

There is a common way of thinking about electromagnetic fields, which is, that they have an energy per unit of volume, and an equal force per unit of area. I read about that when I was looking for lecture notes about electromagnetic fields.

If a static electric field exists, you may assume that the field has the energy per unit of volume and the force per unit of area, but when it is 'static' electricity, you must assume that there are electrical charges to create that field. The field would vanish immediately if there were no electric charges.

If instead you assume that a field is moving at exactly the speed of light, then you do not need to assume that there are any electrical charges. Instead you may suppose that induction of both fields can work without charges. Each of the 2 fields is assumed and believed to induce the other one. At the speed of light an electric field is induced by a magnetic field, and the magnetic field is induced by an electric field, and the two fields can induce each other, as they are moving together and are at right angles to one another.

In the case of ball lightning, it can float through closed windows, and so matter with an electric charge would get stuck and left behind on the outside of the window glass. So electrically charged material could never be a necessary part of the ball lightning structure since it floats through a closed window.

And if it exists without electric charges then you have to assume that its high energy electric field has to be moving at the speed of light together with an equal strength magnetic field, also at the speed of light and at right angles to the electric field.

One may think of a radio wave going through outer space, the wave might have a very strong electric field and an equal strength magnetic field and a lot of energy, but there are no electric charges at all in the completely empty space where it is flying.

So something happens at the speed of light that is not supposed to happen at any lower speed. At all lesser speeds electric fields have to be caused by charges, but at that special speed electric fields do not need to be caused by charges. Enormous numbers of experiments have been done with static electric charges, they have always behaved very simply, and so it's so clear that nothing at all similar to ball lightning could be made with charges.

There is one thing in the electromagnetic field of ball lightning which is completely different from a radio wave: the magnetic field and the electric field in the quickly spinning ball has to point steadily one-way.
 Obviously it can't possibly oscillate or alternate quickly and has to stay one-way.
Its electric field probably points in the radial direction steadily outward from the centre.

I think it is obvious that the fields of ball lightning could never be alternating. I mean could never be oscillating, as the two words mean the same thing. It does somehow resemble a particle, with its round shape, its spinning. Suppose that a small subatomic particle such as the electron were magnified so much that you could see it, would it look a bit like ball lightning?
The ball lightning might be one single particle, but of a different kind?

The important point was that its fields cannot be alternating. If its fields alternated in two opposite directions while they are spinning this would certainly generate radio waves powerfully rapidly with a lot of energy. And it seems impractical for it to keep on losing energy at such a rate if it is going to last for more than a few seconds. Ball lightning has been said to last a few whole minutes sometimes. For several such reasons I feel sure it has a steady field which points steadily one-way.

Witnesses have often said the ball lightning lasted for a few minutes though no energy could have been added to it, which proves that it is stable and it cannot be radiating very much energy as radio waves.

 Holding together, forming a round ball and lasting for so long, even a few minutes is normal for it so there must be a magnetic field pointing steadily one-way, as it might do in some sort of particle. It may have magnetic poles, and something somewhat like an electric charge and especially it is round and spinning.

A first step in creating ball lightning is to filter a radio wave so it stops oscillating and stops alternating, so it stops those things completely and becomes a steadily one-way field.

In a normal radio wave the electromagnetic fields are usually called half-cycles and a train of these half-cycles come one behind the other and give the impression that the wave alternates back and forth in two opposite directions. To something motionless a radio wave passing by has an electric field which oscillates in two opposite directions both transversely to the direction of movement.

 A ball of lightning does not oscillate. There must be a main magnetic field spinning quickly with it at exactly the speed of light, and there may as well be a slower magnetic field extending outside it, and going through its center.

Assuming that it is very much like a radio wave in some ways, the electric field and the magnetic field must induce each other and it is certain that this will cause them to be naturally equal in strength. And just like in a radio wave they must be at right angles to each other, and at right angles to their direction of motion.

So the main part of ball lightning has something in common with a radio wave, in that
1) The electric and the magnetic fields can be considered to be inducing each other, in the way that happens at the speed of light.
2) the electric field and the magnetic field are equal in strength, and
3) they are at right angles to each other, and
4) they are at right angles to the direction of spinning motion which is at the speed of light.

The speed of light lets two fields sustain each other without electric charges

The speed of light is a special speed at which a magnetic field induces an electric field of equal strength to itself, and an electric field induces a magnetic field of equal strength to itself.

I get the impression from reading a little about it, that the two induced fields are also moving at the speed of light so it is a self-perpetuating effect which allows the fields to go a long distance. At the special speed they are able to induce each other, without any loss of strength.
Which I have read makes the two fields together self-sustaining, so they can keep on flying forever through a vacuum or air, a special effect which does not happen at slower speeds.

And though the ball lightning isn't moving it must be spinning at the exact speed of light in spinning motion, so the two fields that make the round ball spinning can induce each other with equal strength, and self-sustain their existence permanently as in a radio wave. Except of course they don't oscillate, they don't have a wavelength, and they don't have a frequency. As they are pointing steadily one-way.

The same effect as works in a radio wave also works in a round spinning ball, the two fields sustain their existence and that could go on forever unless friction removes energy. The friction may be partially that it induces quite small electric sparks, and partially that its vibrations induce glowing light emission in air molecules.

Any vibrations would be due to its not being perfectly balanced, as its being very slightly stronger on one side than on the other side as it spins so quickly, at at least a few hundred million turns a second. It would be like the vibration of a not quite perfectly balanced wheel. Obviously if it were not for friction and vibrations the round spinning ball lightning would be even more stable and maybe last forever.

Ball lightning, and a new polarizing filter

To create ball lightning you would need a high powered radio wave transmitter, producing radio waves with a field strength of at least 1500 volts per meter, and a completely new type and new kind of polarizing filter. The polarizing filter has to conduct electricity in only one direction, and it has to be electrically insulating in the opposite direction.

The electric field of the radio waves alternates in two opposite directions, as usual, but as it reaches the filter parts of the wave that have an electric field pointing one way see the filter as transparent. They fly through it. And the other parts of the radio wave have to be stopped.

This should make a beam of fields which move at exactly the speed of light, but which have an electric field that always points in just one specific direction.

Its state of polarization has gone twice as far as the common polarized state called "plane polarization". And it turns out that when a radio wave is polarized that way it is a profound change.

It has lost its wavelength, it has lost oscillation, it has lost its frequency, and the only thing which it will not lose is its speed of movement, which is still the speed of light. And its energy.

Such a polarizing filter could be made in two completely different ways.

Firstly I want to mention quickly a way that is not that good, not the one I want to use first. It is based on the idea that electrical insulators are usually transparent to radio waves, while electrical conductors are opaque to the waves. An it is based on the idea that when an electric field makes a low pressure gas come close to breakdown, an added electric field in one direction can cause a breakdown which causes the gas to be electrically conducting and opaque. The filter could be made from about 8 long straight low pressure gas tubes physically similar to stroboscope tubes, containing a low pressure gas. And a DC voltage would need to be applied to the two far ends of the tubes just sufficiently to make the low pressure gas become near to electrical breakdown. But not quite breaking down.

It would then be near to, close to breakdown in one direction but not in the other direction since the applied voltage is one direction DC. Unless the gas breaks down, the gas is electrically insulating, and transparent and radio waves will go through it. When the gas breaks down, radio waves would be stopped by it. Of course the electric fields of the radio waves go in two opposite directions, assuming that the waves are the very common plane polarized.

You want the single first half cycle to pass through the filter, and everything after it to be stopped. And because every time this works the single first half cycle which passes through the filter will have an electric field polarized in exactly the same direction, it becomes super-polarized.
Since a DC voltage across the low pressure gas is one-way, the low pressure gas tube can act

differently when electric fields belonging to strong radio waves come to it, depending on the direction of the electric field of that part of the wave.

Plane polarized radio waves are a train of "half-cycles" which follow each other pointing in two opposite directions.

When a short pulse of radio waves starts and then reaches the low pressure gas tubes, its leading half-cycle may be in a direction that will not trigger a breakdown. And this means that its leading half-cycle can pass through the filter, or that is it will pass through the opening which has these low pressure gas tubes as parallel bars over it.

The next half-cycle of the radio waves, will of course always have an electric field in the opposite direction to the leading half-cycle, so it may trigger a breakdown in the low pressure gas, and it will be stopped by that.

There should be no more radio waves during the next few milliseconds, to allow the gas to recover. After a time period of a few milliseconds, the low pressure gas should calm down and return to an electrically insulating state. I have read somewhere that a tiny amount of iodine can make the return to non-conducting happen more quickly.

Just imagine the same thing happening over and over again. And the result should be leading half-cycles passing through the filter always having an electric field pointing in an identical direction. Whereas common plane polarized radio waves have electric fields pointing in 2 opposite directions, these super-polarized waves will have an electric field pointing in just 1 direction, and so they are super-polarized.

About 8 long thin low pressure gas tubes could be arranged like bars in a grid over a window, and the strong radio waves aimed at the window in short separate pulses. The first half cycle in each pulse always passing through the filter. But every other part of the wave gets stopped.

This method have some disadvantages, and I prefer to think about a different method which seems a lot better.

Making a new One-Way Polarizing filter.

The polarizing filter could be made in a different way from chains of microwave switching diodes. To make a filter you need at least 250 to 500 microwave switching diodes. The microwave switching diodes would all be soldered together in several straight chains, and several of the straight chains would be arranged in a parallel grid like pattern over a square opening like a window. They would be placed like parallel bars over a window. So as to form a polarizing filter of a completely new and different kind which you could not have heard of.

The microwave switching diodes can be designed by manufacturers to be able to block or pass microwave frequency currents. What I hope for is that when they are blocking to current, they could be transparent to the radio waves. So blocking to current should mean transparent to waves, since non-conductors are transparent.

It might be necessary to use up to 500 microwave switching diodes. Why so many? Because metal connections between them must be so extremely short that they don't reflect radio waves. It is impossible to use a much smaller number of diodes, and you would need to choose the type very carefully or else some money equivalent to a few thousand dollars could be wasted.
I think that as you chose the type of microwave switching diodes they would need extremely low capacitance, good isolation and very high speed. Especially very high speed is necessary. Choosing the right kind of microwave switching diode should be the only, the only thing in the experiment that is really difficult, it is really the only difficult part, as everything else in the experiment would be fairly easy for someone who has a suitable place in which to do experiments.

The new type of polarizing filter should polarize the radio waves twice as much as plane polarization. When the radio wave is polarized twice as much as plane polarization, it is not actually "a wave" any more, but something which is itself very interesting to science.
There is a comparison you can make, but I should not elaborate on it. In the air you have sound waves and you have wind. Sound waves do not form turbulence, or spinning air currents. A steady wind and gusts of wind blowing one way can produce turbulence and spinning air currents. Especially if you imagine wind blowing past an obstacle like a building or the wing of an aircraft. By the downwind side of a building there can be a lot of little whirlwinds if it is a windy day.
If a strong steady wind blows by a building, there can be swirling air currents at the downwind side and many dust devils.
When a radio wave is polarized twice as much as plane polarization, it is not quite "a wave" any more, as it is now changed and comparable in a sense to "a wind". A comparison to fast flow of air in one direction, is valid, and in its form of turbulence it can form what you might compare to little whirlwinds and spinning fields.
The ball lightning is obviously the only example of a field spinning rapidly which to begin with might have been like a dust devil or like turbulence.

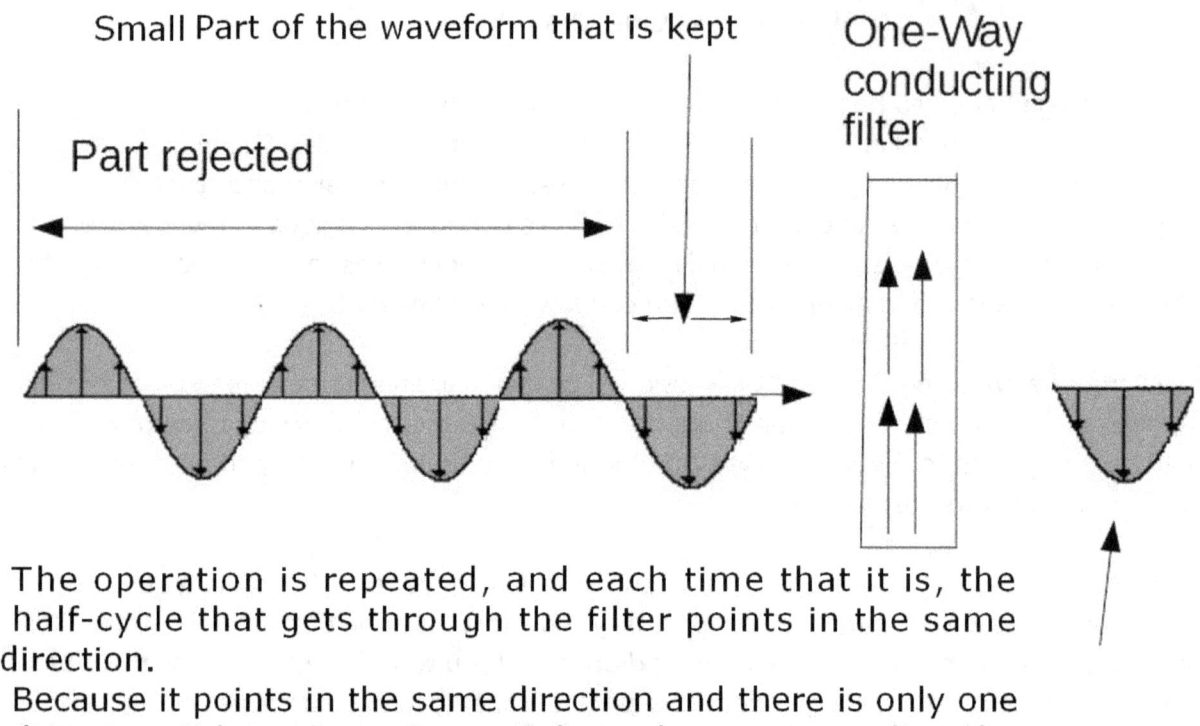

Small Part of the waveform that is kept

One-Way conducting filter

Part rejected

The operation is repeated, and each time that it is, the half-cycle that gets through the filter points in the same direction.
Because it points in the same direction and there is only one direction, it becomes a Super-Polarized wave, extending the concept of polarization

An explanation of the drawing above. A radio wave pulse which has a total length of 3 wavelengths, flies from left to right.

It reaches a very special polarizing filter which lets the wave's 1st half-a-wavelength pass through it. But which blocks and stops the remaining parts of the wave.

You see in the drawing, most of the wave will be rejected. Only the front half-wavelength passes through, and continues flying .

The special one-way polarizing filter is drawn as a rectangle with arrows pointing up.

It would be in reality a square open window that the radio waves can fly through. It would have over the square open window several vertical strings of microwave switching diodes, arranged as a grid shape like a grid over a window.

There should be probably about 50 microwave switching diodes in series along the length of every string in the grid. And about 3 to 8 of those strings would be placed over the window opening. In the drawing, at the right, there is a single half-a-wavelength of the radio wave of a previous pulse. It is the final product which you want to create.

Equipment to create ball lightning

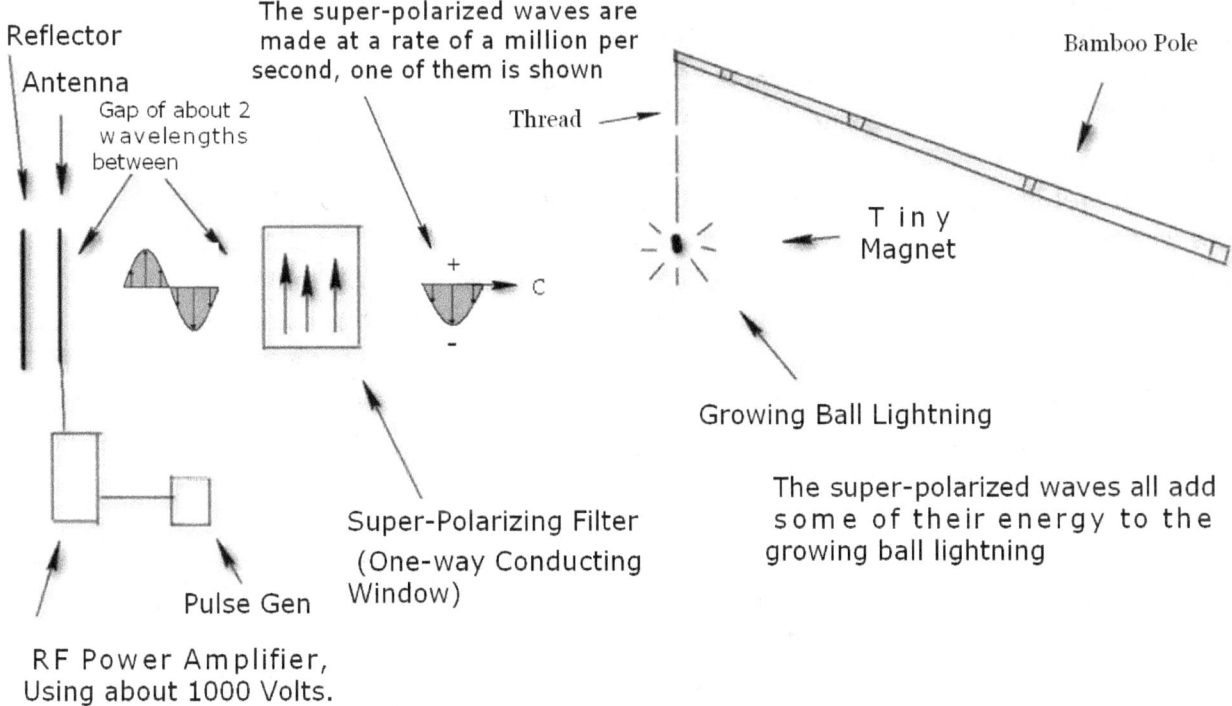

The super-polarized waves are made at a rate of a million per second, one of them is shown

Reflector

Antenna

Gap of about 2 wavelengths between

Thread →

Bamboo Pole

Tiny Magnet

C

+

-

Growing Ball Lightning

The super-polarized waves all add some of their energy to the growing ball lightning

Super-Polarizing Filter
(One-way Conducting Window)

Pulse Gen

RF Power Amplifier, Using about 1000 Volts.

An explanation of the drawing just above:. Looking from left to right: A radio frequency amplifier connected to an antenna, with a pulse generator, makes extremely short pulses of radio waves with a frequency approx 1 GHZ, which is a wavelength of around 30 centimeters. And there may be a pulse repeat rate of approx 1 million a second. Also one should try a frequency of about 500 MHZ, with a pulse repeat rate of approx 100,000 times per second.

Each pulse of radio waves, is the shortest possible length for its wavelength, which means that it is 1 wavelength long. The 1 wavelength long radio waves have 2 half cycles, and it's important the the first of the half-a-wavelengths be very strong. That is achieved by making the pulse generator start suddenly, and by making the amplifier able to work at higher frequencies than the one used. The drawing shows 1 of these pulses. It is traveling from left to right, and very soon it reaches the 1-way filter. The 1-way filter is drawn as a square open window, with arrows over it pointing up. The arrows are to remind you that it conducts electricity upward, but it does not conduct downward.

The pulse of radio wave that reaches the filter, must see it as transparent at first, which means very seriously that there cannot be an electric current flowing in the filter at first.

The 1st half a wavelength of the radio wave pulse, must fly through the filter from left to right.

The 2nd half a wavelength of the radio wave pulse, must be stopped completely by the filter.

The illustration shows on the right of the filter, one of those separated half-a-wavelengths, which is traveling in the left to right direction.

As the pulses each get split in half this way, they would all be identical to one another, and a series of them would be produced at the rate of perhaps 1 million per second, all of them traveling from left to right and all of them with an electric field pointing downwards.

You understand that they are not waves anymore because they do not have a wavelength, their wavelength has been to some extent removed by the fact that all of them have an electric field pointing downwards, all the same way.

They are therefore expected to induce pulsed direct electric currents, or DC. For example, if they pass and reach a loop of electric wire, not shown in this drawing, they should induce DC current. Whether they do or whether they don't induce DC, they should form ball lightning,

There is a tiny magnet hanging in the air, on the end of a thread. The tiny magnet in the air, should act as a nucleus, and the ball lightning should form around it, spinning in the air around it.

More and more energy would be added to the ball lightning which is like charging it up, until it would become visible and glowing. This drawing did not show the ball lightning, but you assume it's in the air around the tiny magnet.

I notice when I look at books, that the "Plane Polarization" seems to be the maximum polarization discussed. Without saying so it seems that scientists might make a completely false and thoughtless presumption that a light wave cannot be polarized more than plane polarization.
If you just think about it when you read this you will see that it's wrong to assume something like that. The light wave may be polarized twice as much, and it is provable that that is possible.

What about a normal radio wave? Within any light wave the individual fields are normally called "half-cycles" or "half-a-wavelength" and coming in a train one behind the other these half cycles point in opposite directions, but if you were to follow a single one of the half cycles you would notice that it keeps pointing in a certain direction which very often does not change, or at least does not ever need to change while it travels. So they are not oscillating, they are steady!
An oscillating electric current is necessary to produce a radio wave in the first place, it launches the fields at the speed of light. But once fields are launched at the speed of light it is its speed of movement rather than a wave like oscillation which allows it to travel far.

The oscillating effect in a radio wave applies to the whole wave seen as a whole, since the individual parts of a radio wave (called half-a-wavelength, or half-cycles) keep pointing in a direction which does not change or at least does not need to change as they travel. I mean that if you followed a half-a-wavelength as it travels, you see that it does not oscillate, as it points in a steady direction that does not change.

I have read that in an electromagnetic wave the electric field is exactly equal in strength to the magnetic field, and the two fields are each though of as carrying exactly half the total energy.
So the electric field carries half the total energy and the magnetic field carries the other half.
The units of measurement used do not make it obvious when the two fields are of equal strength.
An electric field of about 377 Volts per meter is exactly equal in strength to a magnetic field

measured as 1 Ampere per metre. Therefore whenever a radio wave has an electric field of 377 volts per metre, it must have a magnetic field "H" of 1 ampere per metre, since the two fields are in reality equal strength and energy.

Part of my theory is that the two fields inducing each other can happen in the spinning motion of a round ball, as well as in a radio wave, if you assume that the spinning motion of the ball is everywhere moving at the speed of light.

When radio waves pass through some non-conducting substances such as glass which has a dielectric constant, the speed of the waves slows down a little, maybe because the fields are able to induce each other equal strength at the slightly lower speed. Likewise if ball lightning went into a solid block of glass, its spinning would slow down just a little bit, and then if you pulled the ball lightning out of the block of glass its spinning would speed up again.

 I have read that a radio waves' total energy is twice the energy carried by its electric field alone. Also the energy and the force of either field is proportional to its square.
 The electric field and the magnetic field of a radio wave, are thought to store a certain amount of energy in a volume of space.
The energy per volume is proportional to the square of the field strength. One can imagine taking a cube of empty space in a place where there is a radio wave, and with a simple formula calculating the amount of energy stored by the fields in that volume. Both energy in Joules and force in Newtons of any electric field are proportional to the square of its Volts per metre.

 I found lecture notes which said that you should think of taking a cube of volume in empty space and find the amount of energy which an electric field or a magnetic field stores in that volume of empty space.
 I found that there is a simple equation which applies to any electric field, whether it is of a radio wave, or whether it is an electric field between the two widely spaced plates of a capacitor, that connects field strength measured as volts per meter with with two things,
1) a force per 1 square meter area, measured in Newtons, and
2) an energy per 1 cubed meter volume of empty space, measured in Joules.

 I also read something interesting about every electric field and every magnetic field:
Force per 1 meter square area is always equal to energy per 1 meter cube volume.

And I have read that you can think of the field itself as having a force per area and an equal energy per volume, without having to think about electric charges. This idea of not having to consider charges, definitely applied both to the static electric field between plates of a capacitor, which is caused by charges, and to the quickly moving electric field of a radio wave. Which can exist where there are no electric charges at all. It is certainly a good thing that you don't have to think about electric charges. Thinking about electric charges would make it all much more complicated, and so it is useful that the field on its own can be thought of as having both force per area and energy per volume, both of which are always equal to each other.

As for example if a field has a 10 Newton force per 1 square meter area, then it always has a 10 Joule energy per 1 cubic meter volume. And if a field has a 1000 Newton force per 1 meter square area, then it has a 1000 Joule energy per 1 meter cubed volume. Force per area is with no exceptions equal to energy per volume!

I have read in a few university lecture notes that these ideas apply to both the magnetic field and the electric field of a radio wave. And also to the field between the plates of capacitors.
You can if you want to, think of the energy per volume of a field as something belonging to the field itself. Even when the electric field is caused by electric charges, I have read that there is a common way of thinking about it, that the energy belongs to the field itself as it fills a volume of space.
 And that a force per area can be stated for the field. If a field was of extremely high strength, then the field itself would have a very very tiny mass that might be just barely measurable according to the equation $E = MC^2$, rearranged as $M = \dfrac{E}{C^2}$ And you have no need to think about electric charges, which is a good thing as it simplifies things. It is nice that you can think of the pure field itself as having both the force per area and an energy per volume of empty space.
Such ideas should also apply to ball lightning, as its fields must have a force per area and an energy per volume.
;------------------------------------

A Super-Polarizing filter

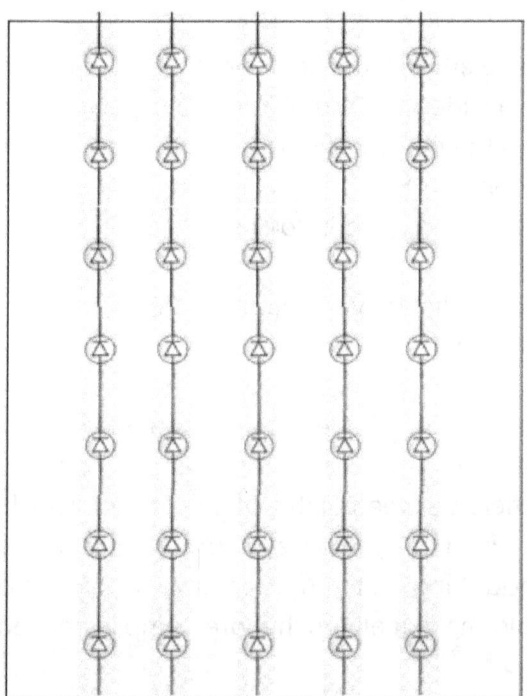

Super Polarizing Filter

The one-way polarizing filter is made from chains of microwave switching diodes.

In this drawing there are only 7 diodes in each chain, but in reality it would be necessary to use more, or maybe 50 diodes in each chain.

Because the metal connections between the diodes have to be so short that they don't reflect radio waves.

← ——————— Metal connections between diodes are too long here, this would ruin it by reflecting radio waves.

The round circles with the little triangles in the middle are of course the symbol for diodes. Though it's not in the drawing, the upper and lower ends of each chain of microwave switching diodes could be connected to electric wires, and a DC battery to give a small reverse bias.

The one-way polarizing filter is the most important part of the whole equipment. And it is supposed to do something which can happen rarely in natural places and natural conditions near a lightning strike in the atmosphere, in the rarest cases during a lightning storm when natural ball lightning is created.

The small round symbols with a triangle in the middle, are supposed to be strings of microwave switching diodes soldered together in series. Obviously the metallic parts between them must be extremely short not to reflect. What I hope for is that when the diodes are under reverse bias, and therefore blocking current, they will be transparent to radio waves. Because non-conductors and electrical insulators are transparent to radio waves.

So when they are reverse biased they should become transparent. And I would hope that when they are forward biased they can instantaneously become opaque and blocking to radio waves.

You would need to do several tests before the experiment can start.

1) Are they transparent to radio waves when the chains of diodes are given a DC voltage which makes them in reverse bias? They have to be transparent in reverse bias.

2) Are they opaque to radio waves when they are in forward bias, and some current flows?
3) Are they fast enough? They would need to switch in amaybe 0.1 nanoseconds from reverse bias to forward bias, and only a few types of microwave switching diode are fast enough.

I have said I think the field of ball lightning is closely related to the field of a normal radio wave, with the one very meaningful difference being that the radio wave has a train of fields following each other which will alternate or seem to oscillate back and forth, while the ball lightning does not alternate, does not oscillate, and must be made of fields that steadily point one-way.

To create ball lightning in an artificial experiment is interesting and the first thing you have to do is to filter a radio wave so that the radio wave stops alternating and stops oscillating, and its fields point one-way. I assume the words oscillating and alternating mean the same thing in this case.

And when the radio wave has stopped alternating, and has stopped oscillating, it has become in that way ready to turn into ball lightning. When a radio wave has stopped oscillating and points one-way, it is then ready to give its energy into forming ball lightning, and I am sure ball lightning can form from it easily, and the ball lightning can have a wide range of different sizes.

And actually from that point onward the experiment becomes easy to do, and it could be quite exciting!

Once you pass a radio wave through the special filter, and the wave has completely stopped oscillating and has stopped alternating, it no longer has a proper wavelength. It might have "something" remaining which depends on the wavelength it previously had? By definition the wavelength is a measure of the distance between two reversals of field direction, and it only has these reversals when it is alternating, which is also called oscillating.
When the alternating and the oscillating has been stopped completely, there is no proper wavelength left in the wave.
Without having a wavelength it is not quite the same thing as a wave. And it has gone a step towards being a little more like something which can be compared to a wind. Of course a wind has its own turbulence and sometimes spinning and vortices especially where it goes past the edge of obstacles.
As you can imagine a wind going past a building and forming turbulence and spinning air currents. Likewise a radio wave which has been filtered so it has stopped oscillating, and points in a single unique direction, may start spinning where it passes by the edge of an obstacle.
Even more interesting, it could be attracted or repelled to motionless magnetic fields, whereas light waves are completely unaffected by motionless magnetic fields. People can look through a microscope at crushed bits of a magnet, and never see any effects of magnetic fields upon light waves, of course.

But I think, though it's not important, a scientist would never say such waves are impossible, because of the very well known theory of Fourier. As it is thought that any repeating waveform of any shape whatsoever can exist and can be made up of a combination of simple sine waves, according to Fourier. Even bizarre shaped waves can be made up from simple sine waves. You just have to find the amplitudes, the wavelengths, and the phases of the component sine waves. Fourier theory must be true.
As any waveform of any shape "whatsoever" can be made from a combination of simple sine waves, so can a wave that does not oscillate at all and that has no real wavelength. Any waveform that points one way for a long time period, contains a component sine wave with almost infinitely long period, probably according to Fourier theory.
 A component with an almost infinitely long period (infinitely long wavelength) seems to mean that in this case the comparison with sine waves is no longer as important as it normally is. I am sure it is not important.
The component sine wave with infinitely long period is like an amplitude that is steady fixed and unchanging, as if it were a half-a-wavelength of a radio wave which has theoretically a infinitely long wavelength! With its infinitely long wavelength, however long you wait, its electric field steadily points one-way! And it does move at the speed of light and yet it will seem as a constant force not to change. And if someone insisted it were a sine wave, it would not matter, and insisting on it might be just a pointless way of saying that the Fourier theory is always true.

I think the experiment with radio waves is somewhat difficult because the special polarizing filter would be difficult to make, and you might have to waste money several times throwing it away and remaking it? Yes you might have to throw it away and remake it with different parts, and waste the equivalent of a few thousand dollars. However, compared to the cost of many other experiments in physics, the total cost would be little.

Imagine a normal plane polarized radio wave whose electric field oscillates up and down, up and down.
You want to make a special filter which removes the parts of the radio wave that have an electric field pointing downwards selectively. How can you make the filter?
The first thing that one thinks of, is the fact that electrically insulating substances are usually transparent to radio waves. And electrical conductors are usually opaque to them.

A filter has to be electrically conducting one way, but electrically insulating the other way.
If a filter was electrically insulating upwards, but electrically conducting downwards, would that filter remove the parts of the wave which have an electric field pointing downwards?

The answer may be, no it wouldn't quite do it that simply. Because once an electric current starts flowing in the filter, it will stop dead all parts of the radio waves, regardless of what direction their electric field points in. Because accelerating and decelerating electric currents reflect electromagnetic waves.
If it did work, the wave would become twice as polarized as plane polarization, and it would not quite be a "wave" any longer.
There is a practical fact: Once an electric current is flowing in the filter, the filter will stop dead all parts of a radio wave, regardless of what direction their electric field is pointing in.
So the filter will only operate correctly and do its job at the start, in the beginning. Since at the beginning no current flows so it can be transparent.
There is a very good practical solution to the problem.
And the solution to that practical problem is to use radio waves in very short pulses. In the quiet period between pulses, the filter can have time to return to a transparent state.

The way to filter a radio wave so that its fields stop oscillating, and stop alternating, and point in a single unique direction only, is to use short pulses of radio waves and aim them so they pass through a special filter that conducts electricity one-way, one-way only transversely to the direction of motion.

This new filter has to be electrically insulating and transparent to radio waves at first when the radio waves' electric field points in the non-conducting direction, and then it has to be electrically conducting and opaque to radio waves whenever their electric field points in the other way.

I think it can be built from several hundreds of microwave switching diodes. Switching diodes are manufactured to have the power to block microwave frequency currents. That is a useful property.

They block the microwave frequency currents whenever a DC voltage makes them in reverse bias. The fact that they can block microwave frequency currents implies that a chain made from many of these diodes might become transparent to radio waves when all are in reverse bias, though of course the metal connections between them need to be extremely short compared to wavelength so as not to reflect the radio waves at all.
They should be linked together in straight parallel chains arranged like a grid. You need to test the filter while a DC voltage puts it in its reverse bias or non-conducting state to make absolutely sure that it is then transparent to radio waves.

To be clear, what I hope is that when the diodes are blocking to microwave frequency currents a chain of them will be transparent to radio waves because the radio wave won't induce any current in them. Hopefully the chain of diodes could act as an electrical insulator.

You need to test your filter before the experiment can go any further. There is a lot here which I don't understand how to calculate. If it were not transparent to radio waves while it is in the DC reverse bias state, you would need to throw it away and buy hundreds of new diodes of another type, which is where money might be wasted. Obviously the metal connections between them have to be extremely short, so short that they don't reflect radio waves. Obviously this is a problem as you know that metal connections can reflect radio waves.

You should also test your filter to make sure that when you apply a forward DC voltage to make a current flow through it, it actually is reflecting and opaque to radio waves.

Of course a test has to be done both ways, one reverse DC bias and test that it can be transparent, the other test with forward DC bias and test that it can be opaque.
When the filter passes both tests, there is still the question about whether it can change at a high enough speed, but I am sure some microwave switching diodes can do it.!

In operation one has to direct at this polarizing filter short repeating pulses of radio waves, with a longer quiet period in between pulses. All the pulses have to be the same as one another. The first half-cycle of a radio wave has to pass through the filter. While all the rest of that radio wave pulse has to be stopped. It has to be stopped because unless it is stopped so as to remove it, ball lightning could not form.

Imagine that the experiment is running. Over and over again the same thing happens, maybe at a rate of several million times per second. And the principle is so simple: Short strong pulses of radio waves are directed at the filter. As a first "half-cycle" of each radio waves pulse passes through the filter and flies forward, it continues to fly forward at the speed of light. And as all the rest of the radio wave behind that first half-cycle is stopped, you can see easily that the part of the radio wave pulses that passes through the filter will every time point in the same direction.

As they come out from the filter they all have an electric field pointing in the same direction, and they all have a magnetic field pointing in the same direction.
This is the principle, both of the fields always point in the same direction every time. There is absolutely no oscillation or alternation back and forth, rather there is a single unique direction in which the fields always point.

The principle is simple. In the electromagnetic field that passes through the new kind of polarizing filter, the electric fields all point in a single unique direction which is the same every time.

So do the magnetic fields always point in a single unique direction which is the same every time. And therefore the alternating and the oscillating has been completely stopped.

There is no oscillating and no alternating left in the wave. But it continues to travel at the speed of light. As normal, the radio transmitting antenna has launched the fields so that they go at the speed of light, and when they can pass through the super-polarizing filter, they continue moving without slowing down. The fields and the energy that pass through the filter must continue moving on at the speed of light exactly, but they no longer oscillate, they do not alternate, and they do not really have anything like a proper wavelength.
As they have no oscillation and no alternation, these fields are ready to create ball lightning.
And in fact making ball lightning from these fields should be a very simple step. The ball lightning continues to move at the speed of light in a round and round spinning motion.

Once you have filtered the radio waves so the oscillating and the alternating is completely gone away, you are 99% of the way towards actually creating ball lightning. And creating ball lightning from that moment onwards is the most simple step: All you have to do is attach a very small bar magnet to the end of a long thread, and using a long bamboo pole or a fishing rod hang the tiny magnet in the air to one side of the beam of electromagnetic fields. Immediately ball lightning should form in the air around the tiny magnet!!

A radio wave half cycle, considered on its own, has a magnetic North side and a South side, as is well known. If the North side and the South side of every half cycle which come out of the filter was pointing in the same direction, then these North and South sides could be attracted to a small bar magnet. The bar magnet would either attract or repel the field depending on which way round it is held.
The fields could then go into circles around it, and then into a spinning motion, spinning around the magnet. It would need room and space to spin in the air which means no cluttering with solid materials. To start with it was moving at the exact speed of light, and with its inertia it would carry on moving at the speed of light, but now in a spinning motion.

You would see a round ball of electromagnetic fields glowing brightly in the air and obviously spinning. If the thread burns up and the magnet drops to the floor, you can try using a fire resistant fibreglass thread. The power of the ball lightning could become very much stronger than the strength of the small bar magnet at its centre. The tiny bar magnet is only intended as a nucleus to start it off, and then to hold it.

If these fields were of really low power, the spinning ball lightning formed would be transparent and completely invisible. You could see nothing, but if you put your hand into the round spinning field you could get an electric shock and perhaps feel heating effects. When the round spinning field is a little more powerful you might see a round glowing light in the dark, something like a round translucent sphere in the air glowing faintly with a light. As the ball lightning forms in the air, more and more energy would be added to it gradually increasing its energy.

Luckily it is more likely that you would be able to produce a strong brightly glowing ball lightning, because in order to operate the new kind of polarizing filter, the pulses of radio waves directed at the filter have to be really strong.
The filter can't work unless the radio waves directed at the filter have an electric field strength of at least 400 to 2000 volts per metre. As minimum.
In practice more and more of the waves that go through the filter will be added to the spinning electromagnetic ball, so over a period of a few seconds it should become brighter and stronger.

Three states of polarization

The arrows show the electric field's directions as the wave comes head-on towards you.

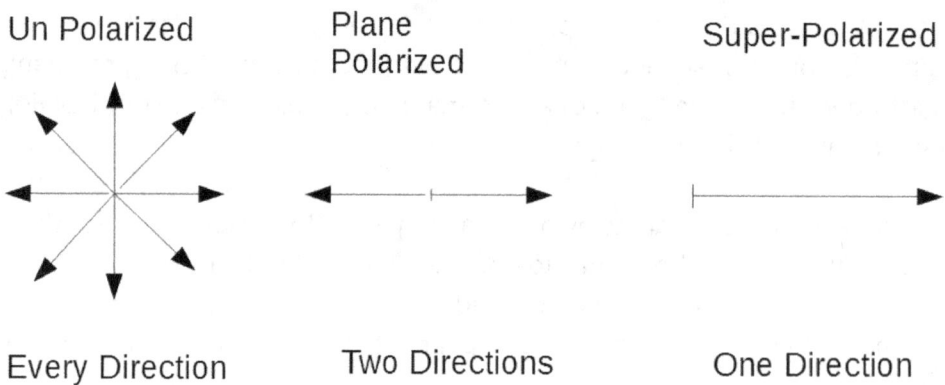

Un Polarized	Plane Polarized	Super-Polarized
Every Direction	Two Directions	One Direction

About the three states of polarization, if a wave points in a single direction it is probably able to induce pulsed direct electric current, or DC? A DC measuring ammeter with a loop of wire would check whether or not it induces DC.

Something About the Idea of Polarization.

This is about creating a new type of polarizing filter which conducts electricity one-way. When thinking about the practical side of it you realize that it is quite impossible for this new idea to work with continuous waves, it can only work with radio waves that are to start with made in short pulses.

Something about polarizing filters, and about the special new kind of filter. You will see that polarization can be carried a step further than plane polarization. To carry polarization a step further than the common plane polarization, is a little bit difficult but the experiment is quite practical.
Ordinary polarizing filters work by either absorbing or reflecting part of a waveform of light and this usually turns circularly polarized light into plane polarized light. Of course it works by removing parts of the waveform and the part of the waveform that gets through the usual filter is called plane polarized.

I have read that one method of creating a normal polarizing filter is to have extremely fine straight parallel metal lines etched onto a sheet of glass. If the lines are too coarse or anywhere near a wavelength it acts as a diffraction grating, but if the lines are very much finer than a wavelength, it acts as a polarizing filter.

I have read that polarizing filters are usually made by stretching a polymer called Polyvinyl Alcohol, so that the molecules of polymer are lined up straight and parallel by the stretching, and then they stain the molecules of the polymer with iodine.
The iodine atoms become attached to the polymer in straight parallel lines because of the stretching which lined up the molecules, and they behave to light as something somewhat electrically conducting in the direction of those straight lines. The lines stained with iodine atoms are very much finer than a wavelength so it works as a polarizing filter.

For microwave frequencies a grid of straight parallel electric wires or thin metal rods can make a perfectly good polarizing filter, as the part of the waveform that induces a current in the metal rods is reflected, while the part of the waveform that has an electric field at right angles to the length of metal rods, flies through the filter. And the microwaves would be changed from circularly polarized to plane polarized.

In any case a radio wave can be emitted by an antenna that is a simple straight wire, and that produces for instance vertically polarized radio waves. The vertically polarized waves are called plane polarized waves. So it is never necessary to use a polarizing filter, as a very simple antenna will do it without any filter. You certainly don't need a polarizing filter to create plane polarized radio waves, as a simple straight wire as an antenna does it.
To create ball lightning you need to polarize the radio wave a lot further.

Some ideas about the technique.

In the normal vertically polarized radio wave, the electrical field of the wave alternates pointing up, down, up, down, up, down, in the two opposite directions. Every radio wave always starts with a first half cycle, and it is then a train of half cycles following each other. All of the half cycles alternate by pointing in opposite directions.

When a radio wave starts very suddenly, then because it started so suddenly it may have a much stronger first half-cycle than it would have if it started more gradually. You need a strong sudden start. In the experiments the first half cycle is the thing you need to keep. While the rest of the wave is considered wasted energy which has to be removed.
In the experiments it implies that the pulses need to start quite suddenly. I think according to what I have read, two accelerations of electric current in the transmitting antenna, one acceleration upward, the next acceleration downward, should be enough to make the right kind of radio wave as a one-wavelength long pulse. And if it is one wavelength long then of course it contains 2 half cycles.

If you use the new polarizing filter to filter the vertically polarized radio waves, you should get from it a new kind of wave, and the extraordinary thing about this new type of wave is that it does not have a wavelength. I repeat: The wave does not have anything that is actually a wavelength.

You need to be flexible, and I fear an unimaginative way of thinking might say a wave has to have a wavelength. There are no reversals in field direction, it has stopped alternating. I thought it might be better called a super-polarized wave or maybe a mono-polarized wave because its fields point in a single direction? And because it is obviously lot more polarized than a plane polarized wave.

As I mentioned it is not quite right to call it a wave, as it does not oscillate, and points one-way.
A super-polarized wave is an electromagnetic field which goes on moving at the exact speed of light though both its electric field and its magnetic fields point one-way. It is different from a radio wave in that it does not have a wavelength, it does not have a frequency, it does not alternate and it does not oscillate.
I assume that the words oscillate and alternate mean the same thing, in this case.

It can go in straight lines, but in the right conditions it should have a tendency to spin around in circles, which actually resembles a wind in the air having spinning as turbulence!
Together with the super-polarized wave there would unavoidably be small amounts of radio wave that remain, because the filtering did not remove them. Including according to the Fourier theory a lot of component sine waves which are there simply because the radio waves happened to be in pulses rather than continuous. Those component sine waves could be harmless to the experiment if they are weak. But they are certainly never a necessary part of the super-polarized wave.
Except for one, a component sine wave which is like an unchanging continual steady amplitude in

one direction. Or I meant something of an almost infinitely low frequency and infinitely long wavelength.

The new polarizing filter has to do something which is simple in principle.
During its actual operation short pulses of radio waves spaced apart by maybe about a microsecond in time, are sent to it. As a strong short pulse of radio waves reaches the filter, it matters that the electric field of the leading half-cycle should be in a direction that sees the filter as transparent.
 So since the leading electric field of the radio wave pulse should pass through the filter, you just make sure you turn the radio transmitting antenna around the right way. The reason why this matters is that once an electric current is flowing in the filter, every following part of the radio wave will be stopped, regardless of whether it points in the conducting or the non-conducting direction.

After every pulse, the filter needs to return back to its electrically insulating and transparent state, and this means that there has to be a quiet period of rest in between pulses of radio waves, which is long enough for the special filter to go back to a non-conducting transparent state.

So the whole idea is certainly simple.
To help the filter be transparent at first some DC voltage can be applied to give the diodes that make it some reverse bias. The moment the **second** half cycle of the radio wave reaches the filter it should immediately induce a current to flow in the filter which makes the filter opaque. This should happen so quickly that the second half cycle is completely stopped, specifically you have to stop the second half cycle.
In order to produce ball lightning the electromagnetic fields of the waves must point only in a single direction, and as the second half cycle points in the opposite direction it would completely stop the ball lightning from forming, and so it must be removed.

So the diodes which the filter is made from need to switch from being electrically non-conducting to being electrically conducting very very quickly, and unless you used enormous out-doors equipment which allows the experiment to be tried out with long wavelengths, the actual time needed to switch from being transparent to being electrically conducting and opaque might be around 0.1 to 0.3 nanoseconds. Therefore there is the difficulty in choosing the right diodes to make it work.
Microwave switching diodes made of GaAs which the specifications say have very low capacitance and good isolation might work. I think the words "good isolation" mean they have the ability to block microwave frequency currents very well. Which is a very important property of the diodes. To make a single filter might need about 500 of the microwave switching diodes. It is impossible to use a much smaller number because metal connections between the diodes have to be so extremely short that they will not be reflecting to the radio waves.

So there should be a repeating cycle with very short length pulses of the radio waves, and a much longer quiet period in between pulses, a quiet period just long enough for the filter to have time to become transparent, and by being transparent become ready for the next pulse.

From the point of view of not wasting energy, pulses of radio waves should be very short. Since only the first half-cycle is useful. And all the rest is not used. Of course once the filter has become electrically conducting and a current is flowing, every part of a radio wave is blocked and that energy is wasted. The proportion of used energy to wasted energy depends on the shortness of the pulses, but actually the proportion of wasted energy is not so important.

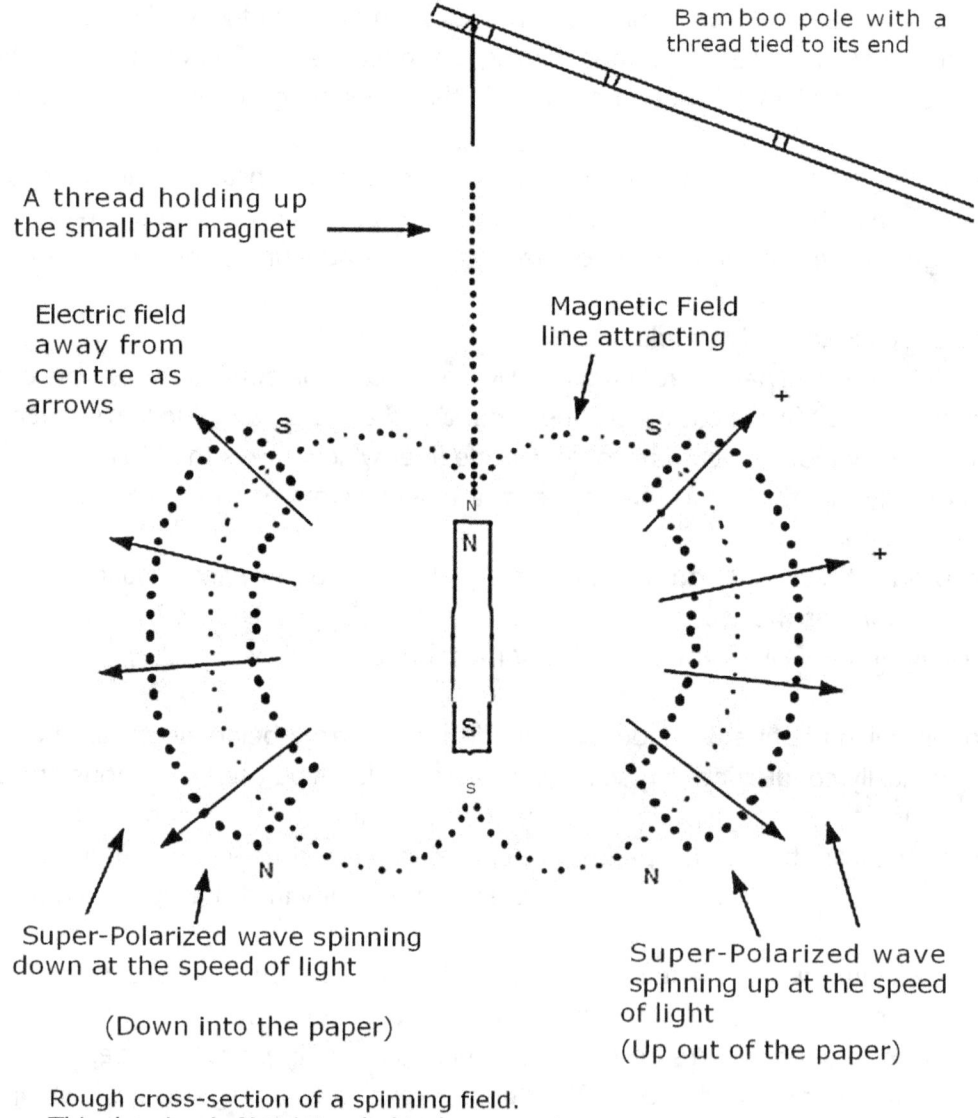

Bamboo pole with a thread tied to its end

A thread holding up the small bar magnet ➝

Electric field away from centre as arrows

Magnetic Field line attracting

Super-Polarized wave spinning down at the speed of light

(Down into the paper)

Super-Polarized wave spinning up at the speed of light

(Up out of the paper)

Rough cross-section of a spinning field.
This drawing is **Not** intended to be accurate

It would be spinning at more than 200 Million turns per second.
The wave went at the speed of light to begin with, and with its inertia it will carry on moving at the same speed while it spins.

As far as I know my polarizing filter idea is all a new idea, and all of the polarizing filters invented in the world so far conduct electricity equally well in the two opposite directions.

Ask yourself what would happen if a polarizing filter conducts electricity in only one direction!

With the start of every pulse, the first half cycle must see the filter as something transparent like a window that it can pass through easily. It has to go on flying ahead at exactly the speed of light. Then it is important that the second half cycle should be stopped as completely as is possible.

What equipment do you need to actually do the real experiment to create ball lightning? Imagine that you have an adjustable pulse generator, making very short pulses of radio frequency current which, must start very suddenly. The frequency, and the length of the radio frequency pulses, and as well, the length of the "off" period in between pulses, should preferably all be adjustable. Imagine that the pulse generator is connected to the input of a very high power high radio frequency amplifier using voltages of about 1000 to 4000 volts, and the output of that connected to a transmitting antenna which is a single vertical rod.
The radio waves themselves will need to have an electric field strength of at least 500 to 2000 Volts per metre!

The quiet resting period in between the pulses would have to be at least several times longer than the "on" length of the pulses. Because the purpose of the "off" period is to let the filter return to a state which is "transparent" to radio waves. For example the length of each pulse could be 10 nanoseconds, and the length of the quiet period could be about 1000 nanoseconds or that is 1 microsecond maybe? It would be an "Off" period of between 10 and 1000 times longer than the "On" period.
It could be important to realise that the "off " period needs to be a lot longer than the "on" period. Every time there is a pulse, the energy that manages to get through the filter is the "first half-cycle "of a radio wave, and these are all identical to one another. So you understand that as they are all identical there is no alternating and there is no oscillating. Oscillating and alternating have been completely stopped by the filter. Since oscillating can only exist if there are reversals of direction, and now they all point the same way.
Only the first half cycle in every pulse matters, you want to get rid of the rest of the radio wave. It's best if the amplifier is capable of higher frequencies than the frequency you actually use, because that higher frequency capability would probably help to make sure that the first half-cycle is strong.

Theoretically the field that passes through the filter cannot know that the rest of the pulse behind it was stopped, because nothing can go faster than the speed of light and so that information can't catch up with it. This is an important fact, the super-polarized waves cannot find out that the wave

behind them was stopped.
 And most important, the part which passes through the filter will have an electric field and a magnetic field both pointing in an identical direction every time!

Now in a practical experiment you need to wait a while for the electric current in the special one-way filter to die down and stop completely, and for the filter to return to a transparent state, ready for the next pulse. That might take maybe a microsecond, or a few microseconds.

Minimum power necessary to operate the filter?

To operate the super-polarizing filter, the radio waves which reach it need to have a minimum voltage of maybe about 600 to 2000 volts per metre, because the filter could be made from chains of many microwave diodes soldered together in series. And diodes have something called "a forward voltage drop," which is often 2 Volts per diode with GaAs diodes. And the forward voltage drop means that they won't conduct electric current at all, until the voltage applied across them is at least a bit greater than their forward voltage drop. As a large number of the diodes are in series, the forward voltage drop adds up.

This forward voltage drop can actually be useful as it absorbs energy and turns the energy into heat in the diodes. For instance, if 100 diodes are in series in one chain, the forward voltage drop of the chain would be 200 volts.

In the experiment the new polarizing filter has to be transparent when the first half-cycle of the radio wave comes to it. The first half-cycle flies through the filter without hindrance, and continues to fly on.

And then immediately after that, the new filter has to conduct electricity and stop dead the second half-cycle of the radio wave. If the forward voltage drop were very low, you would hope that the filter will reflect all of the second half-cycle.

But because of the high forward voltage drop, you have to hope that the new filter will absorb a lot of energy from the second half-cycle. To absorb energy efficiently, the ratio of forward voltage drop to the radio waves' electric field voltage, should have a certain best value. I really don't know how to calculate the best value. But I think you can assume that when the electric field of the radio wave at its peak is, 4 to 10 times greater than the forward voltage drop, a lot of the energy of the second half-cycle would be both absorbed and reflected which would help it to work.

4 to 10 times 200 volts would mean that the radio wave needs to have an electric field of maybe 800 to 2000 volts where it reaches the filter. In cases when the radio waves are much too weak, the new filter would absolutely not work at all.

The forward voltage drop of the diodes in series, is the reason why the radio waves have to have a very powerful electric field. The electric field of the radio wave has to be several times stronger than the sum of the forward voltage drops which all the diodes in one chain have in series.
 The need to make metal connections so extremely short compared with the wavelength that they are not reflecting, means that each chain of diodes might need to contain about 100 diodes in series.

If the radio wave has too little electric field strength, the filter could not possibly work.

A question is, what power would the radio wave have to have to have this voltage? I found two formula which connect voltage of a radio wave with its power. With P=power density in watts per square meter, and E= electric field in Volts per meter, $P=\dfrac{E^2}{377}$ Or that is $P=\dfrac{(Volts/Meter)^2}{377}$

The other formula was $P=\epsilon_o E^2 C$ Where P is the power of a radio wave in watts per square meter and E^2 is the square of the electric field strength in volts per meter, and C is the speed of light in meters per second, and Epsilon is the permittivity of free space constant $\epsilon_o = 8.854 \times 10^{-12}$.

Obviously if both formula can give the same result, then $\epsilon_o C$ must be the same as $\dfrac{1}{377}$ And a check with my calculator shows that $8.854 \times 10^{-12} \times 300 \times 10^6 = 0.002656$ while $\dfrac{1}{377} = 0.002652$ so they are almost exactly the same.

So according to either of these two formula, if the radio wave had an electric field strength of about 377 volts per meter, it would have a power density of 377 watts per square meter.

To have an electric field strength of twice that, or 754 volts per meter, I think it would need a power of about 1,508 watts per square meter. If the radio waves needed a field strength of 1000 volts per meter, I think this would require a power of 2,652 watts per square meter.

To operate the filter radio waves of field strength from 600 volts per meter to 2000 volts per meter might be just barely enough.

Maybe this means that the pulses of radio waves would need a peak power of approximately 1,500 to 5000 watts per square meter where they reach the filter. This is essential simply to make the filter work as the filter cannot possibly work when the radio waves are too weak.

And it is because the radio waves' own voltage needs to be several times greater than the forward voltage drop which all the diodes in a chain have in series so that the second half-cycle can immediately induce a strong electric current in the chain and this has to stop dead the second half-cycle.

But the average power would be much less than the peak power. As the "off" period might be roughly 100 times longer than the "on" period. So, a necessary pulse power of 5000 watts per square meter might mean an average power of only 50 watts per square meter or so? The average power would definitely be much less than the "on" power.

,---------

Here are some ideas which might be relevant to ball lightning as they are about fields.
I have read that the force per unit of area of an electric field is always equal to its energy per unit of volume.
Unit area meant 1 meter square, and unit of volume meant 1 meter cubed. The same thing is true for a magnetic field. The force can be measured in Newton. By definition 1 Joule of energy is 1

Newton-Meter, the mechanical energy when something pushes for a distance of 1 Meter with a force of 1 Newton.

A force of 1 Newton is defined as the force which gives a mass of 1 kilogram an acceleration of 1 meter per second per second. Therefore a Newton is approximately 100 grams of force.

So thinking about a cube of empty space with 1 meter sides, you can understand that if there is a force of 1 Newton acting on the 1 square meter of one side of that cube, and that pushes through the cube's depth of 1 meter, then this uses 1 Joule of energy. And this must be the reason why the energy per volume of a field is always exactly equal to the force per area of the field.

I read something about the field between the widely spaced apart plates of a large parallel plate capacitor. If you imagine that the 2 plates are separated by 1 meter distance, and there are opposite electric charges on the two plates which attract each other.

Thinking of a 1 meter square area of both plates, within a much larger parallel plate capacitor. Though the field in between the two plates is caused by electric charges, I read that it is possible to think of the energy as something belonging only to the field in the volume of space between the two plates, and you do not need to actually think about the electric charges.

When the two plates are mechanically moved closer together, the volume of space in between the plates is used up and disappears at the moment when the plates meet. The amount of mechanical energy you get when the plates are mechanically moved closer together, is exactly the same as the electrical energy the field is thought of as storing in the volume of space.

I thought it was interesting that I have read that whenever the area of the two plates is much greater than the distance between them, changing the distance between the plates does not change the amount of attracting force in Newtons caused by charges. The attractive force stays constant because of geometry, while individual point charges on their own feel less force with the square of distance. To try to explain it I believe that when the two plates are moved 10 times further apart, 100 times more area containing charges is there roughly in the direction perpendicular to the surfaces of the plates. The multiply by 100 cancels out the divide by 100, so the force remains constant.

I have read that if the plates are moved closer together, the energy stored in the electric field between the plates is gradually used up in exact proportion to the volume of the field that is gradually used up to disappear as the plates move closer together and meet. (On the other sides outside the two plates there is almost no electric field.)

And that must be why a fields force per unit area is always equal to its energy per unit volume.

I read that exactly the same ideas about force per area being equal to energy per volume, that apply to the electric field of a capacitor also applies to the electric field in a radio wave, which is thought to carry half the total energy of the radio wave. And I read the same idea applies to the radio waves magnetic field which carries the other half of its total energy.

And the radio wave field can of course give you exactly the same amount of energy whether it gives up the energy mechanically or electrically.

This is something very important to think about, it is in well-known physics, and it's the equivalence of electrical and mechanical energy.

If you think of a 1 meter square window somewhere close to a transmitter, then because the radio wave moves at about 300 million meters per second, you can think of a volume of fields of 300 million meters cubed as blowing through the window every second.

The volume of a radio wave passing through a 1 meter square window, has to be about 300 million cubic meters every second. (at the density it has where it passes through the window).
Its total energy is spread out over that 300 million cubic meters, and diluted that much.

And if you think of static electricity having a natural weak force, and think of comparing it to the electric field of the radio wave, you can imagine that each cubic meter of the field has a mechanical force per 1 meter square area which, if it worked pushing or pulling something for the 1 meter depth gives you the energy which the field stores in that 1 meter cubed volume of space.
The energy in just 1 meter cube is of course 300 million times less than the energy going through 1 meter square window each second.

For example, if the power of the radio wave passing through the 1 meter square window was 300 watts, then the energy in 1 meter cube of its field would have to be 1 micro-joule. And its force over a 1 meter square area would have to be 1 micro-Newton.

If the power of the radio wave passing through the 1 meter square window was 300 Kilowatts, then the energy in every 1 cubic meter of the field would be about 0.001 Joule, and the force of the field on an area of 1 square meter would have to be about 0.001 Newton. (About 0.1 grams of force.)

If the radio wave was extremely powerful, or about 300 Megawatts a square meter, then each 1 meter cubed would store 1 joule of energy, and the force per 1 meter square area of the field would have to be 1 Newton, (about 100 grams force) since energy per volume is the same as the force per area.
Actually I have read that the electric field of a radio wave is considered to carry half the total energy, and the other half is carried by the magnetic field. So each of the two fields needs only half the force.

So in the case of the 300 kilowatts per square meter, the electric field should have a force of 0.0005 Newton per square meter, and at right angles to that on two other faces of the cube, the magnetic field should also have a force of 0.0005 Newtons per square meter. (About 0.05 grams of force). Though the force of any radio wave seems very small, that must be simply because the energy is spread out diluted over a very large volume of field.

As said if a radio wave passes through a 1 meter square window, its volume where it passes through, must be 300 million cubic meters per second, and if you think of that it helps understand the equivalence of electrical and mechanical energy.

In the ball lightning the fields would not be spread out or diluted like it, because all of the fields which gave their energy to forming the ball lightning would be added up, and as if wrapped around the center, and superimposed on each other, inside the relatively small space of the sphere shape.

So forming a field that is actually really strong. It isn't like the radio wave in which the fields are so spread out over very large areas. Instead the fields which added their energy to the growing ball lightning are superimposed on one another in the small volume, and constructively added to one another making energy concentrated in a small volume.

When ball lightning gets created in the experiment, super-polarized fields would come out through the special polarizing filter at the rate of maybe a few million per second, depending on the timing between pulses.

The timing which you would want to adjust depending on how long it takes for the new polarizing filter to become transparent again. A certain proportion of these fields which you might imagine as maybe about 50% to 5%, would get added to the growing ball lightning. As fields are added to the growing ball lightning they would always naturally be superimposed one on top of the other making the ball lightning stronger.

It seems likely that the ball lightning naturally has a force per area equal to its energy per volume.

So that the equivalence of electrical and mechanical energy works for ball lightning, just as it works everywhere else.

So whenever it stores a lot of energy its fields will have a very strong force per area. The ball lightning's fields could even have a force of hundreds of kilograms or of tonnes.

In nature a really strong ball lightning might sometimes have a force of tonnes per one square meter area.

 If that is the case no wonder balls of lightning sometimes make a bang when they explode. I assume they had a very strong force per area, and that could have helped make them explode quite loudly.

The electric and magnetic fields should always be about equal strength, and they could sometimes have a force per area of a few hundred kilos force or even several tonnes of force per 1 square metre.

If it explodes, the explosion would be in many cases a change in direction of the field, from spinning in a circle to flying out and going in a straight line for some distance.

Then if the field starts spinning again, a secondary ball lightning would appear from the explosion some distance away, and in many cases there could be a whole cluster of secondary balls of lightning which appear when the first one explodes.

Energy that was spinning suddenly goes out in straight lines almost and travels for a distance in straight lines. The change from spinning in tight circles to going out in straight lines is the explosion and I suppose you would hear a loud bang, and dangerous fields could fly around. You could use a screen of wire netting to protect yourself, because the fields could easily embed themselves deeply inside your body, and cause serious burns.

The only explanation I can think of for why the ball lightning which floats calmly does not induce strong electric currents in the air, was that its electric field might maybe point evenly and uniformly away from its centre with an about equal strength all over. If that is the case there is no loop in the plain air around which an electric current would want to flow strongly. And in that case its extremely strong electric field would merely produce effects similar to static electricity?
Plus the fact that it would vibrate as it spins.
  Forces per area of hundreds of kilograms or even tonnes per square meter are possible when the ball lightning has enough energy. Any strong forces are only possible you assume if there is something that prevents the energy from being lost quickly, as it would be lost quickly if there were a violent electric current. The strong electric current would not happen if you assume that the electric field points evenly outward from the centre with equal strength all over, which means there is no round path along which a current could be induced. It would prevent strong electric currents from forming immediately and short-circuiting the energy.

A form of cancelling out that might take place with normal light waves, hasn't been considered. But without this cancelling out light waves could possibly have attraction or repulsion with magnetic fields? Cancelling out could mean that scientists do not know some of the properties of electromagnetic fields. Cancelling out is something that may happen in light waves because of their reversing of field directions.
With normal radio waves the constant alternating of fields that follow each other pointing in opposite directions might cancel out some physical properties. And these physical properties might not be noticed by any physicists because they were always being cancelled out. Super-polarized waves might let you see some physical properties which have not been measured before simply because they were always being cancelled out whenever people experimented with radio waves.

Such as, these fields might be deflected by electric and magnetic fields. Though normal radio waves are not deflected in the slightest tiniest bit by magnetic fields, these super-polarized waves might be deflected by a small bar magnet. Other properties might also be revealed which are cancelled out in radio waves, and it would be rather new to knowledge of physics.

This is a diagram of the one-way polarizing filter, the radio wave on the left and the super-polarized waves on the right. The strong pulses of radio waves coming from the left should have a strong first half cycle. Its first half cycle is shown just to the right of a vertical dotted line, and behind that dotted line the rest of the wave will be blocked by the filter.

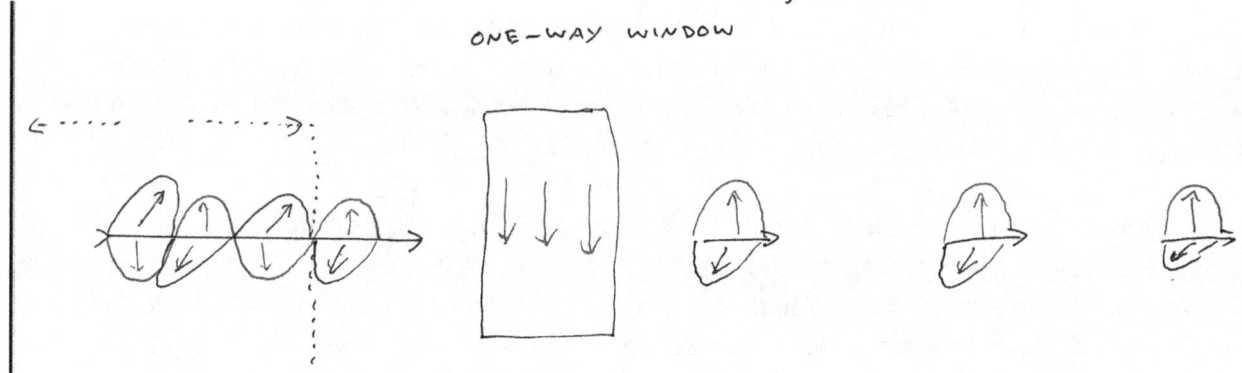

ONE-WAY WINDOW

The First Half-Cycle in each pulse of the radio waves sees the filter as something transparent and therefore it goes through, but everything after the first one is stopped. The filter is not ready for the next pulse until it has rested and become transparent again.
 Arrows on the one-way filter show which way it is electrically conducting. In an upward direction it must be non-conducting and transparent. In a downward direction it must be electrically conducting and completely opaque.

On the right hand side of the new polarizing filter you can see three of these isolated half cycles, identical to each other, which have been able to get through the filter, and they will fly further at the speed of light. Actually they would be spaced a lot further apart than it appears in the drawing.
 They are now super-polarized waves, and they should no longer be called half-cycles, since there is now no cycle with them, and they will all point in a single same direction. And there is no real wavelength left.
So wavelength has almost disappeared, oscillating and alternating has vanished, and so while it moves at exactly the speed of light this is a new form of electromagnetic field. It has nothing that is exactly like a wavelength because the concept of wavelength depends on reversals of field direction and alternating quality. (Of course it does have a distance between pulses, but that is not really a wavelength. Theoretically gaps could be filled in to get something continuous.) There are no reversals of field direction, and oscillations have completely vanished, there is no wavelength.

The drawing is not meant to be accurate, and in reality they would be spaced much further apart from each other because each of them came from a separate pulse of radio waves. And so they are really separated by the time period between pulses.
Theoretically the gaps between them have no meaning as they could be partially or completely filled in by aiming at the same spot beams coming from separate sets of equipment.

I mentioned that I think some properties should exist which are cancelled out in normal radio waves. One I though of is perhaps being deflected by normal motionless electric and magnetic fields, something which never happens with normal light waves or with radio waves. [If you imagine looking at crushed bits of a magnet under a microscope, the magnetic field is never visible since magnetic fields do not bend light].

Super-polarized waves would tend to naturally travel in curves or spin in circles when the conditions are right.

The following idea is a possibility of something that might help them to travel in circles?

When something has a north and a south magnetic sides, lines of magnetic field normally form to join the north side to the south side. The electromagnetic field of a radio wave called a "half cycle", does have a north side and a south side, and that is clearly illustrated in many textbooks.
But of course the half cycles of radio waves alternate and point in opposite directions.

Suppose that the waves fly past the edge of an obstacle like a small sheet of metal. If new lines of magnetic field began forming somewhere else like the shadow area behind an obstacle, to join the north side to the south side, what about the second radio wave half cycle which would come with its usual pointing in the opposite direction? As it comes pointing in the opposite direction, that magnetic field which was just beginning to form would vanish. It might begin forming and always be cancelled out?
Because the next half cycle would always have a north side and south side pointing in the opposite direction.

If a magnetic field bends the super-polarized waves, and if they are able to increase the strength of the same magnetic field which attracted them, maybe this state could self-perpetuate, and end up causing a spinning field with the new waves spinning in a circle.

 In the case of a turbulent spinning wind or a dust devil there is a lower air pressure in the centre, and the amount of energy that goes into the spinning motion gets increased a lot by the law about conservation of angular momentum. Its conservation increases the kinetic energy that a spinning thing has when the radius of the spinning circles becomes smaller. The angular momentum concept can apply to anything spinning including ball lightning. I wonder if there is anything at all in plain electromagnetic fields which can be compared to a lowered air pressure?
  Obviously when you have actually made ball lightning you can try experiments to try to find out what gives it its perfectly round shape.

This is another rather poor drawing of the super-polarized waves in simplified style. They are travelling from left to right at the speed of light. In reality they would be spaced further apart from each other. The super-polarized waves have an electric field "E" pointing one-way, and that they have a magnetic field "M" pointing one-way and at right angles to the electric field. Though at the moment they are travelling in straight lines, they are able to form a spinning field.

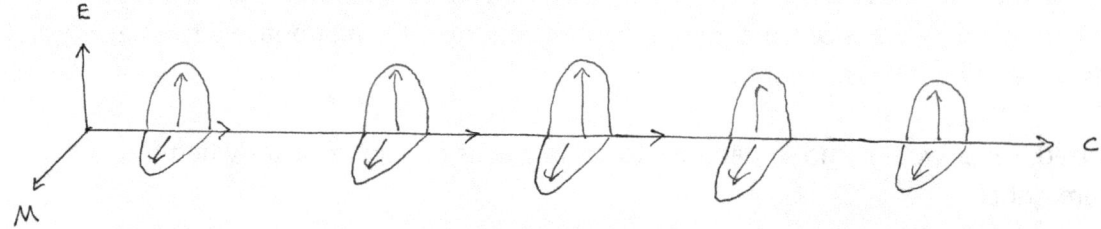

If you stood in the way of these waves they would give you an electric shock. The electric shock danger might be a lot worse than it is from radio waves that have similar energy, and so as you experiment you would need to use a long pole to reach into the super-polarized waves without giving yourself a strong electric shock.

The half-cycles of a normal radio wave are made of both an electric field and a magnetic field which are always at right angles to each other, and always at right angles to their direction of motion. And the two fields are always equal in strength, and they are each thought to carry exactly half the total energy. Their electric and their magnetic fields are always in step with each other. The usual name "half-cycles" is not a very good name for them. The name seems to wrongly imply that there has to be a cycle.

If you followed a particular half cycle and keep looking at it alone, you would not see any oscillations, you would see that the half-cycle steadily points the same way all along. The fields that point up continue to point up, the fields that point down continue to point down. So these fields can keep their directions while they move forward.

So with the normal radio wave the word "alternating" applies when you think of the train of half-cycles following one another, and is not true of the individual fields isolated on their own.

The shortest of all radio waves is believed to be one wavelength long, and it contains only two half cycles. (One wavelength could contain four quarter cycles if it were circularly polarized.)
The two half cycles have electric field and magnetic field vectors pointing in opposite directions, so the wave as a whole alternates.

The half cycle is like a basic building block from which a wave is made, and a one wavelength long wave is simply two of those building blocks. So the half cycle is actually more interesting, more fundamental than the wavelength which is two half cycles.

One way to make the new type of polarizing filter is to use chains of about 50 microwave switching diodes soldered together in series, with the chains arranged in a parallel grid pattern over a square opening which would be about 1 or 2 wavelengths wide. And the other way of making the filter would be to use a grid of long and straight low pressure gas tubes similar to stroboscope tubes but with a DC bias voltage applied so they break down more easily one way than the other way.

You have to send very strong short pulses of radio waves at the filter. If you do it and the filter works you have created the field which can then turn into ball lightning. You could not stand in the field because it would give you a severe electric shock. The danger of electric shock could be many times worse than it is with radio waves of a similar power. A safe way of doing the experiment is to have a long bamboo pole and to reach into the field of super-polarized waves with the end of your long pole.

If you hang a very small magnet on the end of a thread, you can hang the tiny magnet in the air and safely move it about in different areas of the field of super-polarized waves.
 The tiny magnet hanging from a thread would start off the process of forming ball lightning. Ball lightning should form very quickly after that. I think it is a way of immediately forming ball lightning.

You would simply hang a tiny magnet in the air, tied to the end of a thread, and hold it up with a long bamboo pole, and try hanging it in different positions at the sides of the beam of super-polarized waves. The super-polarized waves are moving at exactly the speed of light to start with, and with their inertia they should carry on moving at the same speed as they spin in circles.

And a tiny magnet might not be necessary after all, because a small plastic ball given a static electric charge might start off the formation of ball lightning as easily as a tiny magnet.
So one should also try using a static electric charged ball hanging from the end of a thread.
Obviously if the tiny magnet or a small ball with a static electric charge is hanging on the right hand side of the beam of super-polarized waves, the ball lightning which forms around it would have a clockwise spin direction, but if you hang the tiny magnet on the left hand side of the beam, the ball lightning which forms would have a counter-clockwise spin.

Obviously many positions would work, but it would probably not form ball lightning if it were hanging right in the middle of the beam, because it is probably impossible for ball lightning to have both a clockwise spin and a counter-clockwise spin at the same time.

Whether the ball lightning has a clockwise spin or a counter-clockwise spin could affect things like whether the ball lightning has an electric field pointing towards its centre, or pointing the opposite way away from its centre. In other words, is the ball comparable to a positive or a negatively charged thing? It could affect what electric charges can gather in the centre of the ball? I wonder, how much do electric charges accumulate in the centre of a ball of lightning, and is that at all important? The direction of spin and electric charge could affect how strongly two balls of lightning explode when they meet each other.

It's an interesting possibility that if the tiny magnet were spinning, this might help the ball lightning to form more easily? You might try to spin a tiny magnet with an electric motor and see whether spinning the magnet makes a lot of difference?

An experiment could be to use an electric motor to spin a tiny bar magnet along its long axis, and see whether ball lightning which forms round it becomes more powerful than when the magnet is not spinning.

Of course its spinning would be very very slow compared to the speed of light at which the super-polarized field spins, but spinning the small bar magnet even slowly could still have an effect. The beam of super-polarized waves could give you a strong electric shock if you stood in it, it might be deadly. So to experiment safely you should tie a thread to the end of a long bamboo pole and use the long pole to reach safely into it.

I think one of the reasons why super-polarized radiation might give worse electric shocks than radio waves, might be that in water and the human body electric currents are carried by the movement of ions. Ions are massive and have inertia, and the very quick change of direction in the electric field of radio waves might to some extent decrease the effect on the ions.
As super-polarized radiation has an electric field always pointing in the same direction every time it comes, it could maybe give ions in the human body more movement, against their inertia. So for example if you stood in the way of a beam of super-polarized waves that have a strength of 500 volts per metre, it might give you an electric shock as badly as touching a 500 volt bare wire.

Another experiment is a little bit difficult to do: The tiny magnet hanging on the end of a thread can be an electromagnet. If first ball lightning formed around it, and then if you then turned a switch to increase the strength of that tiny electromagnet which is now at the centre of the ball of lightning. Then as an ice skater spinning pulls in her arms and spins faster, that could draw in the ball lightning, make it smaller and increase its kinetic energy quite a lot.
I mean the law of conservation of angular momentum would make the ball lightning more energetic when you increase the magnetic field pulling the spinning ball lightning inward.
I suppose that as the spinning field is attracted more strongly to the tiny electromagnet at its centre, it contracts, and because its angular momentum is conserved while it contracts, its kinetic energy should increase a lot making it a more powerful but smaller ball of lightning.

A good question is, knowing that the electric fields of all the super-polarized waves point in a single direction, will the waves induce DC or direct electric currents? I am not sure but I think super-polarized waves can induce strong DC currents, and not AC.

When the equipment is switched off the ball lightning should continue to exist for a few minutes.

I am thinking that natural ball lightning sometimes lasts for a few minutes. And if you find the right conditions the spinning field might even last for ten minutes while no extra energy gets added to it.

The size of the tiny magnets would not be related to the size of the ball of lightning which could form in the air around it, and other things would affect the size. But you want the magnets to be very small in comparison with the size of the ball lightning so that they don't create friction against the spinning part of ball lightning, which could wear out its energy. Probably if the magnet was large the ball lightning would rub against it and so lose energy too quickly.

Now if you do it with 2 long bamboo poles and 2 tiny magnets attached to the ends of the poles with a thread, then depending on whether it is hanging in the air to the left hand side or on the right hand side of the beam of super-polarized waves, the ball lightning which forms will have either a clockwise spin direction or a counter-clockwise spin. Then the interesting experiment is to bring the two balls of lightning together while they have opposite spins, or equal spins, to see what happens when they meet.

And when the two balls of lightning of opposite spin directions touch each other there might be a bang of a rather powerful explosion generating a burst of radio waves. To be safe you would need a wire mesh shield in front of your head to protect yourself from burns, as in the explosion new balls of lightning might be formed which would sometimes fly through the air very quickly. I suppose that when new balls of lightning are created by the explosion they might fly away at speeds of up to half the speed of light!

If a ball of lightning flew and got embedded deep inside your body it would burn you, but a shield of metal wire mesh should keep it away. Definitely balled lightning could go deeply embedded in your body, causing burns.

;----------

Centrifugal force of ball lightning

When something spins you feel the centrifugal force pulling outward. Centripetal force is equal and opposite to the centrifugal force and is always pointing in to the centre. The centripetal force is a real force, whereas the centrifugal force is sometimes called a tendency to fly apart because everything wants to travel in straight lines.

It is said that the only force necessary to keep something moving in a circle, is the one force, a centripetal force which always points towards the centre of the circle. Without the centripetal force it would fly outwards in straight lines and immediately break up. In ball lightning something has to somehow attract the fields toward the centre and so something can make the centripetal force.

I think that in the case of anything at all which is spinning there is a centripetal acceleration in meters per second per second, which is $\dfrac{V^2}{R}$ with V a velocity in meters per second and R the radius in metres. Because in the case of ball lightning the velocity V is C the speed of light, the centripetal acceleration $\dfrac{C^2}{R}$ is certainly very high since $C^2 = 90,000 \, million \, million$.

The speed of light squared! The centripetal force is always mass times acceleration. Though the acceleration is extraordinary, in this case the mass is also extremely small, extraordinarily small. Its mass is determined only by the energy in the ball lightning and Einstein's equation rearranged $M = \dfrac{E}{C^2}$. You notice that the speed of light squared increases centripetal acceleration but the speed of light squared also decreases the mass. The result is simple, C^2 above and below the line of the fraction cancels out. $\dfrac{E}{C^2} \, x \, \dfrac{C^2}{R} = \dfrac{E}{R}$ Is the mass times the acceleration. The force which is needed to create this mass times acceleration is merely E over R.

I did a very rough calculation to find out whether the field strength of ball lightning, acting over an area, could be sufficient to overcome centrifugal force, and create the centripetal acceleration needed to keep it spinning in a circle or a ball shape.

The result of a very rough calculation was that it certainly is possible. Though I do not know any of the details of how the fields can cause a round ball shape, which means that something attracts the fields to the centre.

;------------------

The very important difference between the fields of a radio wave and ball lightning, is that a radio wave alternates, for example up and down, up and down, whereas the ball lightning field does not alternate at all, and on the contrary it points steadily one-way.

The super-polarized waves also point one-way, and they obviously have a north side and a south side, and whenever anything has magnetic north and south sides, you would expect magnetic lines of force to form in the air to join the north and south sides.

If magnetic lines of force form in the air around the outer sides of a beam of super-polarized waves, as you might expect, the fact that each wave points in the same direction as all the others means these magnetic lines of force would not get cancelled out. They might even get stronger each time another super-polarized wave comes along, if a lot of them keep arriving.
In the case of a normal radio wave, the alternating of half cycles that point in opposite directions would cancel it out so well there would be none.

If the super-polarized waves were flying in a curve, lines of magnetic field might form joining their north and their south sides along the inner radius of the curve. This might possibly make their flight path bend into a smaller curve, and fairly quickly turn into a spinning field.

The field of ball lightning moves at the speed of light and is quite identical to the field of a radio wave except that all of it points one-way, with a north side and south side which stay pointing in the same direction. Its pointing one-way and steadily staying one-way, is the specific way that it is different from a radio wave. The ball lightning's field must be the same as a part of a radio wave In most other ways, being different from a radio wave only in that it never alternates but points steadily one way.
;------------

As the wave which points one-way meets an electrical conductor it should induce a DC current, and the magnetic field which will rise around the electrical conductor should repel the wave.

A surprising fact is that the natural ball lightning does not induce very strong electric currents in the air, even though it must have a really strong electric field. You guess that it does not induce a strong current, because the induction of strong electric current would drain away the ball lightning's energy quite quickly. A ball lightning which induces strong currents would probably lose energy so quickly it would end with a bang. And even if it had loads of energy that would be used up in a second.

But people who have seen ball lightning sometimes say the ball lightning lasted for several minutes, while you must assume no more energy is being added to it, proving that nothing in the air drains away its energy quickly. As it lasts for several minutes with no addition of energy the same thing will happen when ball lightning is created artificially.

The only explanation I can think of for it not inducing strong electric currents while it is in the air, is that the electric field may point outwards away from the centre, with a uniform and even equal strength everywhere. If the strength of its electric field were exactly the same uniform everywhere and pointing away from the centre, then it would not induce electrical currents no matter how strong its field. Because there is no loop of a circuit in that case. It would induce electrostatic effects, but not strong currents.
In this case by "electric field" I meant the electric field which moves at the speed of light while the

whole ball spins, and which has to be at right angles to a magnetic field that also moves at the speed of light, and as they both induce each other. Which is all similar to a radio wave except that field directions are not alternating, but is pointing one way. So probably this electric field points radially outwards from the centre.

But it glows brightly, and I think its very strong electric field is not quite the same everywhere and as it rotates so quickly at a billion revolutions per second it vibrates. And its electric field's vibrations at some frequency somewhere near 200 MHZ to 4GHZ might be able to stimulate air molecules to make them emit light. Possibly it does also induce tiny little electric currents too, forming an area where there is lots of little sparks?

The first step in the experiments is to make a special polarizing filter which is an electrical non-conductor in one direction, which is quite transparent to radio waves in one direction. But which conducts electric current in the opposite direction. You would aim short pulses of very high power radio waves at the special one-way filter. The first part of each radio wave would fly through the filter, because it sees the filter as a non-conducting transparent window.
It is the first half-cycle of the radio wave that sees the window as transparent and gets flying through the window. While every part of the radio wave after it is stopped.

I have described a very clear idea of how you could do it. For a technical reason it won't work with continuous non-stop radio waves, but that is not a problem since it should work very well with short pulses of radio waves.

When your special polarizing filter works, you should be able to create ball lightning in a second and do it over and over again.!
And you would be able to create balls of lightning of many different sizes. I don't know what would determine the diameter? Some spinning in a clockwise direction, some spinning counter-clockwise, and the direction in which it spins can be decided very simply. And you might bring them together to see whether they explode or interact when they approach and come near each other. Moving any small piece of metal into the ball lightning might make it explode loudly, especially when the piece of metal is magnetic.
Such an explosion is obviously not an explosion of matter, but of energy changing into a slightly different form.
Individual balls of lightning would certainly come with two different electric field directions.
They can either have an electric field which is positive on the inside, negative on the outside, or with negative on the inside and positive on the outside.
When two ball lightning with opposite electric field directions come together and meet, they might very well explode more powerfully than if their electric fields point the same direction, and their energy might be converted back into radio waves. It would mean in the explosion a very powerful but short burst of radio waves.
Also they might splatter and produce more secondary balls of lightning some of which might float

free, and some of which might shoot across the room quickly? If a ball of lightning flew across a room quickly and it got embedded inside your body, it would give you severe burns, and so you should have a shield of wire mesh to make it safe.

It is certain that a ball of lightning could get embedded deeply inside your body and it could cause electrocution and deep burns. A screen of wire mesh in front of you should make it safe.

Experiments done so easily with them would open a new field of physics.

;--------------------------------

How is ball lightning created naturally? I have an idea. When lightning strikes there is at first a very strong radio wave, and then something which separates two half cycles in one wavelength in that radio wave.

And which is unusual, the natural ball lightning probably comes from a single radio wave half cycle on its own, not from more than one in this case. It is possible for it to be created by merely a single half-cycle of a radio wave, because the radio wave emitted was high in energy.

So high in energy that just one half of one radio wave cycle, contained all the energy that the ball lightning needed to form and to be visible.

When lightning strikes its electric current is millions of amperes, and so it can emit a very strong pulse of a radio wave, and it's this radio wave that's important because it turns into ball lightning. In rare conditions that are just right the air could act as the special one-way filter which filters radio waves. Because the air close to the lighting often has a strong DC electric field across it,. The air nearby to lightning can by chance be nearly ready to break down and conduct electricity.

This thing was called "avalanche breakdown", and when it is close to happening, a small extra electric field can trigger the avalanche breakdown. The radio wave itself would have in it that extra electric field that can trigger the avalanche breakdown if the air was already coming close to breaking down. But avalanche breakdown is triggered one-way since the electrostatic field in stormy weather can be vertically one-way across the air. Such as positive charge above with negative charge below perhaps.

The strong radio wave pulse emitted by the strike of lightning, will of course always have a first half cycle, with an electric field pointing in an opposite way to the way that could trigger avalanche breakdown. The first half cycle does not trigger avalanche breakdown. According to usual rules of induction the radio waves' first half cycle would often be with an electric field in the opposite direction to the direction that would trigger avalanche breakdown.

The first half cycle of that radio wave will therefore not trigger avalanche breakdown, and so it will fly through the air finding the air transparent. It will fly on ahead through the transparent air and go a certain distance, perhaps a long distance, but not necessarily very far as its field may start spinning and form the ball lightning.

But the second half cycle of the same radio wave, will immediately trigger avalanche breakdown in the atmosphere, and this will stop it. Stop it from passing through the air, and so, the air acts as a filter, allowing the first half cycle of a radio wave to pass through it, but stopping completely the

second half cycle of the same radio wave. The result is a separation of half cycles.
The air acted as a filter that allowed the first half cycle to go through it, but which then stopped the rest of the wave.
The half cycle that gets through the transparent air and is not stopped, creates ball lightning.
The half-cycle that was stopped would have prevented ball lightning, so it is lucky it was stopped.

The rest of the emitted radio wave would have inhibited, cancelled out the formation of the ball lightning, and so it needed to be stopped and removed. (It is a little bit comparable to sound waves versus winds, since sound waves can't form a whirlwind, but large scale winds can.
A radio wave is compared to a sound wave. And a separated half cycle is compared to a wind for obvious reasons. If you imagine a wind blowing hard, where there are some obstacles that it blows around, it can form little eddies and spinning air like whirlwinds. But, if a sound wave were causing the air to blow an extremely short distance back and forth that would never be able to form eddies or whirlwinds since each direction of back and forth air movement would tend to make an opposite direction of spin.)
 In any case the second half cycle of the radio wave would have inhibited the formation of ball lightning, and avalanche breakdown removed it.

The case of artificially creating ball lightning will be different. It would not be necessary for a radio wave to have extreme power, and more and more energy would be gradually or constantly added to a growing ball lightning.

When super-polarized waves are created they would add their energy to growing ball lightning, they can easily constructively interfere, and superimposed on each other and interfering constructively, they would add up to charge up the ball lightning to higher and higher energies. At the rate of maybe one every microsecond, more and more of the identical half cycle fields that flew through the one-way window and have become super-polarized waves, would be added together increasing the energy of the ball lightning. It would store energy and last for maybe a few minutes after all the equipment is turned off, gradually losing energy.

A formula to do with electromagnetic fields.

The fields of ball lightning must be so closely related to the fields of radio waves, that if you can understand anything about the radio waves that might help to understand something about ball lightning. I found something interesting. Firstly there were websites where you can calculate the relationship between the power of a radio wave and its electric field strength.

Something interesting is that electric fields and magnetic fields are both considered as storing an amount of energy in a volume of empty space. This energy is considered to be stored in the field alone and you do not need to include any electric charges in a calculation. Also an electric field or a magnetic field is considered to have a force per area which is measured in Newtons per square metre. And it's not necessary to include anything at all about electrical charges in a calculation of either force per area or of energy per volume, since you can just state the fields strength in volts per metre.

The same simple formula can be used for either the static electric field between the plates of a parallel plate capacitor, or for the electric field component of a radio wave though that radio wave moves at the speed of light. The same simple formula gives the field's energy per unit volume, and the field's force per unit area. Both are always equal numbers and found by the same equation. A unit area is 1 meter squared, and a unit volume is 1 meter cubed.

With the fields, energy per volume is always equal to force per area.!
The electromagnetic field in a radio wave is considered to be both an electric field and a magnetic field of equal strength and at right angles to each other, and they can have a force measured in Newtons per square meter area, and an energy measured in Joules per cubic meter of volume, and that is simple since it does not involve electrical charges.
The energy stored by an electric field E per unit volume of empty space is proportional to E^2 the square of the field strength, where E is measured in volts per metre. For the magnetic field energy stored by the field per unit volume of empty space is also proportional to H^2 the square of the field strength. Where H is measured in amperes per metre.

The same simple formula gives a radio waves' energy per volume and force per area (both are equal) and this energy depends on the square of the field strength, with the radio waves' electric field carrying half the total energy and the radio waves' magnetic field carrying the other half of the total energy.
The radio waves' magnetic field can be measured several ways, including as amperes per meter H. Because the unit of measurement is different, a radio waves' magnetic field only looks different from the electric field on paper, though actually they both have exactly equal strength.
A very simple formula shows what electric field strength in volts per meter is equal to a magnetic field in amperes per metre.
$$\frac{E}{377} = H$$

If you can calculate the force per area of a field and the energy per volume in space of a field without involving electrical charges that simplifies things a lot, and it's better that way. It's actually essential that you do not involve electrical charges when you think about ball lightning as it's just a field.

Energy per volume and force per area of electromagnetic fields

Of course in physics books, the electromagnetic fields which the radio wave is made of are often called "half-wavelengths", or "half cycles". When the light wave is circularly polarized you can say there are "quarter cycles" too. In one wavelength of the circularly polarized light, there can be 4 quarter cycles, such as, right, down, left, and up for example.

It is interesting that the energy is thought to be stored in space by the field itself and not by any electric charges which might be causing the field.
Of course when a radio wave is in completely empty space its two fields are inducing each other, and at that specific speed the two fields can induce each other without any electric charges ever being necessary.

The electric and magnetic fields are believed to store energy in space which is related to the amount of mechanical work which they can do. If there is a cube 1 meter wide and 1 meter deep in space, the force which the electric field in it has on a 1 meter square area, can move something with that force over the 1 meter depth, doing as mechanical work the amount of energy which the field was considered to store in a unit volume of space. A unit volume is 1 meter cubed. The field is then perhaps considered to have vanished now that its energy has been used up. (In definition the energy of 1 Joule is the work done by a force of 1 Newton moving a distance of 1 metre.)

The equation of energy stored in a unit volume of empty space by an electric field is $\frac{1}{2}\epsilon_o E^2$
Where E is volts per metre, and the epsilon symbol is the permittivity of free space,
$\epsilon_o = 8.854 \times 10^{-12}$. The force per area is always equal to the energy per volume.
And so the same simple equation gives you two things at once, and the two are equal. It gives you the force per 1 meter square area, and it gives you the energy per 1 meter cubed volume. For a
magnetic field, an equivalent formula is . $\frac{1}{2}\mu_o H^2$ and this gives simply both the energy stored by the magnetic field in a 1 meter cubed volume of space, and the force of the field per 1 meter square area.

The constant μ_o was called the permeability of free space, and $\mu_o = 4\pi 10^{-7}$
If the letter A is the area in square meters, then the force of an electric field over the area A must be in Newtons $\frac{1}{2}\epsilon_o E^2 [Area]$ And the energy which an electric field is considered to store in a volume of empty space must be $\frac{1}{2}\epsilon_o E^2 [Volume]$

Equivalent formula for the magnetic field is $\frac{1}{2}\mu_o H^2 [Area]$ to give the force on an area, and
$\frac{1}{2}\mu_o H^2 [Volume]$
to give the energy a magnetic field stores in a volume of space.

It seemed to me surprising that the connection between an electromagnetic field's energy per volume and force per area is so simple. Luckily it is not necessary to think of electric charges when thinking of a field having a force per area.

I suppose the professors who figured these things out must have been thinking of the concept of mechanical work. An electric field produced by anything in empty space can do either electrical work or do mechanical work by its attraction force, and in both cases the amount of energy is exactly the same and the field seems to vanish when it has done its work. The energy of an electromagnetic field in a volume of space can do either mechanical work or electrical work with an equal amount of energy emitted.

I read that you don't have to think of the electrical charges to find either the force or the energy. I read that it is enough to think of a field alone.

The energy of a field in a 1 meter cube volume of space is considered to be the same as the amount of mechanical work which the field could do. (A Joule is 1 Newton-metre, and it is the energy of something moving through a distance of 1 meter with a force of 1 Newton.)

As the radio wave flies past you, a very large volume of that wave goes through a rather small area, just because its speed is 300 million meters per second. Consider a radio wave flying through a window that is 1 meter square in area, a volume of 300 million cubic meters of the radio wave will pass through that window per second.

So if 1 meter cube of volume of the radio wave, had an energy of 1 micro-Joule, you know 1 micro joule sounds like a very small amount. But then since 300 million cubic meters of the radio wave pass through the window each second, the energy per second of the radio wave would then be 300 watts. And the force of the radio waves' field over a 1 meter square area would be 1 micro-Newton. (About 0.1 milligrams.)

But if 1 meter cubed of the radio wave had an energy of 1 Joule, the radio waves' energy through the 1 meter square window would be 300 megawatts. And the force of the radio waves' field over a 1 meter square area would be 1 Newton, or about 100 grams.

I think this probably means that a 300 megawatt radio transmitter pushes away with a force of about 1 Newton or 100 grams? Half the thrust would be from the electric field and the other half of it would be from the magnetic field?

If you think of a 1 meter cube in space, 1 Newton force pulling over a depth of 1 meter is 1 Joule energy, and it is maybe interesting that a force of about 100 grams pushing over a distance of 300 million meters is 300 megajoules too.

Both force per unit area and energy per unit volume, depend on the square of the field strength, so that when a radio wave has 10 times the field strength, it has 100 times the energy. As a radio wave spreads out from the antenna and its energy per area decreases with the square of distance, its electric field strength decreases only in direct proportion to distance. It must be because a tenth the field strength would mean a hundredth the energy.

The rule that energy is proportional to the square of field strength must for sure be true for ball lightning, since it must be made from a very similar type of field as the half-cycle of a radio wave. Assume that a radio wave has been filtered so that its magnetic field points in a single unique direction and so does not alternate, this can be done in practice. It is somewhat less wave-like, and it is slightly to a degree more like matter and a bit less like a wave.

Physics textbooks explain that light and radio waves are made from an electric field and a magnetic field which fly at the speed of light, about 300 Million Meters per second. They store energy in a volume of space, their electric field strength can be measured in volts per metre. Their magnetic field strength can be measured several different ways, including as amperes per metre. When an electromagnetic field is moving at the speed of light, its electric and magnetic fields are considered to be inducing each other and this makes them be always equal in strength. (The inducing of each other must mean that they self-perpetuate without any electric charges ever being there.)

In the case of the air, an air wave that does not oscillate at all is a wind. In the case of an electromagnetic field, the super-polarized waves simply do not have anything that is actually a wavelength. You need to be imaginative to agree that waves do not always need to have wavelength. A wave that has no wavelength is slightly less like a wave and more comparable to a wind, which in this case has a movement of a plain fields at the speed of light.

 The most obvious question to ask is, if the electric fields all point in the same direction, will the wave induce DC direct currents in electrical conductors?
It's the obvious question, and I think they probably do.

;---------------------------

Now an ordinary polarizing filter for light waves, can be a disc of glass with an extremely fine grid of electrically conducting lines etched on its surface, that are straight and parallel. The grid of parallel electrically conducting lines simply needs to be much finer in size than the wavelength of the light used, and it will act as a polarizing filter.
 I read that common polarizing filters are sometimes made from a polymer whose molecules have been stretched in one direction, and then which has been combined with Iodine. The Iodine atoms stain the straightened polymer molecules creating a grid of parallel lines which is to some extent electrically conducting.
A normal polarizing filter for radio waves, can be simply a grid of some straight parallel metal wires.
 You don't need the normal polarizing filter, since a simple antenna made out of one straight wire will emit vertically polarized radio waves anyway.

Now if you have vertically polarized radio waves to work with, physics textbooks would be wrong if they claimed the idea that it cannot be polarized to a greater extent.
The waves can be polarized more. The normal vertically polarized radio waves' electric fields may

point up, down, up and down, obviously in two opposite directions.
Suppose that you could simply delete all the electric fields which point down, leaving those which point up?

And obtaining a radio wave where the electric fields all point one way, in some single direction, with those pointing the opposite way having been deleted. Well it is obvious that this would be polarization going further than normal. But has anyone thought carefully about whether it is possible or how to do it?
In practice the new type of polarizing filter should work with short pulses of radio waves. But the end result can be the same, it is not a problem that you have to start with short pulses.

When the radio waves have passed through a filter so that their electric fields all point in a single direction, they are in a state of polarization which goes a step further than usual, and in this further state of polarization the wave obviously will not alternate any more.
It has no oscillation, and no back and forth movement with anything like alternation. Instead it is certainly a one way field, but there are gaps.
 It is a radio wave which has no oscillation left in it at all. It has then become slightly less a wave, and ever so slightly more like something new you haven't heard of.

I hope it is possible to make the polarizing filter from microwave switching diodes. They are manufactured to have the power to block microwave frequency currents.

This drawing shows only directions of movement. It just supposes that like winds in the air, a barrier might cause a little bit of swirling? And where there might be some swirling, in the shadow left by a barrier.

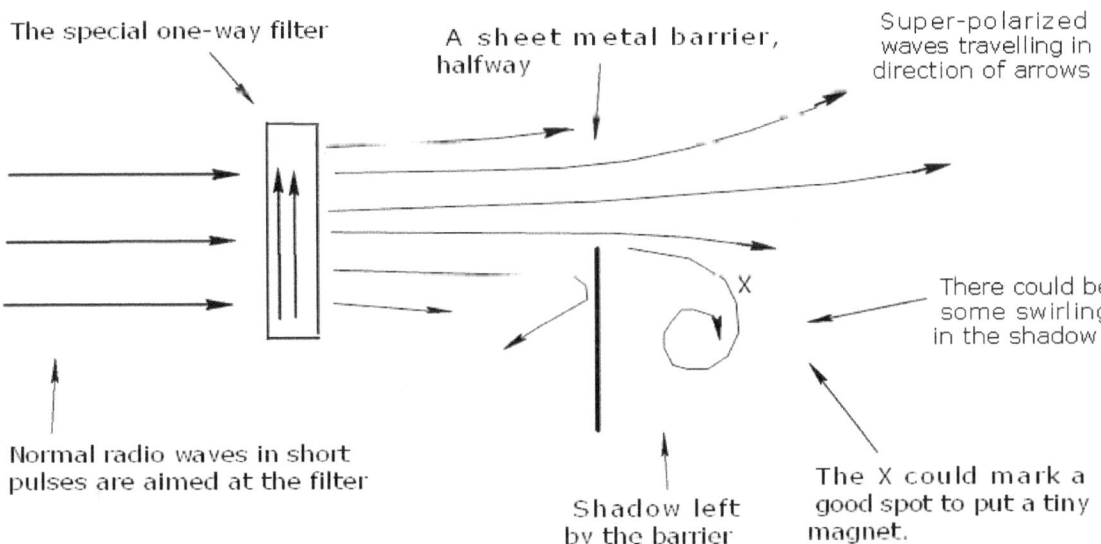

The special one-way filter

A sheet metal barrier, halfway

Super-polarized waves travelling in direction of arrows

Normal radio waves in short pulses are aimed at the filter

There could be some swirling in the shadow

X

Shadow left by the barrier

The X could mark a good spot to put a tiny magnet.

Some tests on the filter.

The parallel chains of microwave switching diodes would be like a grid, with narrow empty spaces between them. You would want the air spaces to be somewhat narrow compared to the wavelength to prevent the radio waves from leaking through the gaps, and so somewhere between 4 and 10 of these chains of diodes would be necessary for the square window opening of the filter. I don't know how many of these strings are really necessary to prevent leaking? But you need to test that by using plain straight pieces of stiff metal wires instead of the diodes, for just a minute. And if too much radio wave energy leaked through gaps between them, then you would know that the gaps should be more narrow to prevent leaking.

In each chain of diodes, about 50 to 300 microwave switching diodes should be soldered together in series, so that they are in a straight line which can be placed over the 1 or 2 wavelength wide window or opening.

Obviously metal wires would be much too reflecting and if there were only a few diodes in a chain the metal wires joining them together would be longer and so they would be a lot too reflecting. Longer metal connections would unfortunately stop the first half cycle from passing through by completely reflecting it.

I think about 50 to 200 diodes in series would be necessary in each chain.

Simply because you want the metal connections between diodes to be so short that they do not reflect radio waves.

Luckily the microwave switching diodes have actually been manufactured to be able to block microwave frequency currents, which implies that their capacitance is low enough.

Obviously when they are blocking to currents, they can be transparent to radio waves.

A DC voltage causing reverse bias must be able to make the window become transparent.
A DC voltage giving forward bias must be able to make the window become opaque.

You need to test the special polarizing filter window using a DC voltage both ways, with 2 tests.

Firstly a test with DC voltage giving reverse bias, to make sure the filter becomes transparent.

Secondly another test with DC voltage giving forward bias, to make sure the filter becomes opaque.

When the filter has passed both tests, it is still not quite certain that it is going to work, because, it must be able to change from transparent to opaque at a high enough speed. And in real operation it would need to change from transparent to opaque in less than half a nanosecond.

After you have done both tests, the real operation of the window could be started. In its real operation, you need to use very short pulses of very high power radio waves, while there is some milder DC reverse bias, and you have found the amount of reverse bias that is just enough.

The change from transparent to opaque should take less than a quarter of a nanosecond from the instant when the radio waves' second half-cycle comes along and with its electric field causes a forward bias voltage. This seems to me like a problem. If the diodes cannot change from non-conducting to well-conducting in a time period equivalent to less than about an eighth or a tenth of a wavelength, then they are not fast enough since the second half cycle of the radio wave might not be completely stopped, and it has to be stopped.

As a result you should get fields moving at the speed of light but oscillating has completely gone away, and the waves have none of what you might call alternation and oscillation, since they are all pointing in one single direction.

It goes a step further than the polarization which is described in the physics and electronics textbooks.

I believe that as soon as you create strong fields which are super-polarized in this way, you will be able to create ball-lightning almost immediately and the ball lightning would be able to form ever so easily. The ball lightning would be a spinning field of electromagnetic force always spinning at exactly the speed of light.

The idea is that at the special speed of light two fields, a magnetic field and an electric field can induce each other and continue to exist for any length of time without there being any electric charges to produce them. Which does not happen at slower speeds.

You want to know the field strength that ball lightning would have, supposing it stores a specified amount of energy. Its field strength per stored energy should be similar to other electromagnetic fields, such as radio waves.

I spent some time looking up radio waves on the internet. Looking for things that I felt applied to both radio waves and to ball lightning, but I only wanted the non-mathematical or very simple mathematics. And I found some interesting things. The most interesting were two equations for connecting the field strength measured in volts per meter to the energy stored in an electromagnetic field in Joules per cubic metre.

In lecture notes I found it is clearly said that electromagnetic fields store an amount of energy in a volume of empty space, and the energy belongs to the field itself. It was interesting that you can think of it in such a way that the energy does not belong to electric charges, it belongs to the electric field itself, which stores energy in a volume of empty space.

The professors who wrote the websites wrote something about "unit areas", and "unit volumes", and that simply meant areas of 1 square meter and volumes of 1 meter cubed.

In order to calculate the energy stored in a volume of space by an electric field, it was not necessary to include the electric charges that might cause the field. In an electromagnetic wave, it is assumed that the field itself has a force per unit area (measured as Newtons of force over 1 square metre) and an energy per unit of volume in space (measured as Joules of energy per 1 meter cubed of volume).

What makes these formula relevant to ball lightning, is that you never need to include an electrical charge in these formula, you can just say the strength of a field in volts per metre and from that find both its force and its energy without anything to do with electric charges.
;-----------

I believe witnesses have really seen that ball lightning is able to float gently through solid things like closed glass windows, closed plastic windows and sometimes brick walls. And that shows it must be merely a field of force, and as a pure and simple field of force it has very little or no charged matter as a part of it.
Or maybe it has an amount of electrically charged material which is very very small in proportion to its energy and in proportion to its field strength.

I have read that if an electric field is moving more slowly than the speed of light, it has to be made by electric charges. And a magnetic field moving more slowly than the speed of light has to be made by moving electric charges. The field would obviously vanish as soon as the electric charges go away.

But when the two fields are moving together at the speed of light, it is not necessary for there to be any electric charges to maintain the fields. In a radio wave in space the pair of electric plus magnetic fields does not need any electric charges to continue to travel through space and exist permanently.
So the speed of light is special, because it allows electric and magnetic fields to exist together without any electric charges, as it happens commonly with a radio wave in space for example.

The facts that ball lightning can float calmly through solid glass windows, a solid obstacle and a barrier to matter, shows that it is a field and that there are no electric charges in its necessary parts since the charges would be stopped by the solid obstacle of the glass windows.
So I think only at most an extremely small proportion of ball lightning's fields can be made by electric charges, and nearly all of its fields have to be moving at the speed of light so that they are able to continue to exist without electric charges by inducing each other in a way that only happens at a special speed.

Radio waves emitted from an antenna decrease in power with the square of the distance, but I have read that their electric field strength measured as volts per metre decreases in direct proportion to distance because the energy in an electric field is proportional to its square. Which is why the formula have E^2 in them for square of electric field. For example a field of 10 volts per meter is 100 times more powerful than a field of 1 volt per metre. The same is true for a magnetic field.

As a radio wave is emitted from an antenna, there is something around the antenna called a near field and further away a far field. The near field is very close to the antenna and it maybe decreases with the cube of the distance, and it is not actually the radio wave, but it must be helping the actual radio wave to form.

The far field is the true radio wave, and the far field starts to be relatively pure at distances of maybe at least 2 wavelengths away from the antenna.   (In the experiments I thought about, the one way filter has to be in the far field only, so there has to be a minimum distance of perhaps I hope 2 wavelengths.)

Some antennas transmit energy equally in all directions, and they are called isotropic. If an antenna is slightly directional then the antenna's gain is often the comparison of its power in the stronger direction compared with an isotropic antenna which transmits equally in every direction. If an antenna has a gain "g" written as decibels as Dbi, then this gain is only the measure of its ability to be somewhat directional compared with the isotropic antenna.

When an antenna is isotropic, so it transmits equally in every direction, the radio waves coming out from it expand in shells of a shape like spheres and therefore have the surface area of a sphere, which is, $4\pi R^2$.

As the radio waves flies away from an isotropic antenna its total power is divided by the surface area of a sphere with radius R equal to the distance d meters from the antenna. So the total power is divided by $4\pi d^2$ to get the power per square meter at a distance d.

 When you move further away from the transmitter, the energy per area must decrease with square of distance but the field strength decreases directly with distance because energy and force in the field is proportional to the square of the field strength measured in volts per meter.

For example a field of 100 volts per meter has 10,000 times more energy than a field of 1 volt per metre. The same thing is true with the magnetic field.

 The total power of an isotropic transmitter is divided by that $4\pi R^2$ surface area of a sphere to get a power per unit area. The total power in watts was called P_t . For example when the isotropic antenna transmits 100 watt of power, then at a distance of 10 meters the wave has spread into a sphere of area $4\pi R^2 = 12.566 \times 100 = 1256 \, M^2$ and its power per 1 square meter area is $\dfrac{P_t}{4\pi R^2}$

which is in this case $\dfrac{100}{4\pi 100} = \dfrac{100}{1256.6} = 0.0795 \; watts\_per\_square\_metre$.

In an electromagnetic wave the electric field and the magnetic field each carry exactly half of the total energy. The electric field is always equal in strength to the magnetic field, and they are always in step with or that is in phase with each other. As the waveform goes past you, its peak power at an instant of peak is exactly twice its average power. I found the formula which connects the electric field strength measured in volts per meter with the force of the field per area and with the energy per volume.

Something interesting was that "force per area" and "energy per volume" are both exactly the same number! They are calculated by the same simple formula. A professor on a website called them force per unit area and energy per unit volume, but actually the word "unit" was not quite necessary and the formula would work with any area or volume.

 By definition energy of 1 Joule is the work done by a force of 1 Newton moving over a distance of 1 Metre. The fact that the energy per volume and the force per area are the same number is simple and must be connected to the idea of the field doing mechanical work.

I have read that regardless of whether an electric field is between the plates of a parallel plate capacitor, or in space as part of a radio wave, the electric field can give up its energy either to do electrical work or to do purely mechanical work. The amount of work is exactly the same whether its form is electrical or mechanical. If you imagine a sort of cube in empty space, containing an electric field, 1 meter square sides and 1 meter deep.

The cube might be a volume between plates of a parallel plate capacitor? Or it might be just a place where there is a strong radio wave in space? The electric field can have a force which acts on the 1 meter square area of the side of that cube, and it can pull two opposite sides of a cube or the plates of a capacitor together with that mechanical force until its 1 meter depth is used up.

At that moment two plates meet so there is no more volume between them, the field is used up. So the field could pull with its "force per area" until the 1 metre depth of that volume is used up. This must explain why force per area is equal to energy per volume.

Pure radio waves do not seem to have a strong mechanical force, but actually they have a mechanical force that is proportional to their energy per volume of space. It seems small because the energy is spread out through a very great volume. Diluting it through the very large volume makes it seem mechanically weak. As for example the radio wave passing through a 1 metre square window has in that place a volume of 300 million cubic metres in a second.

The amount of energy that the radio wave has in just one of those cubed metres, is actually proportional to a mechanical force which the field has on a 1 square metre.

Ball lightning is concentrated in one place. It is not spread out in the way of a radio wave, since all of its fields that it's made from and that have added energy to it, are superimposed one on top of the other. As energy gets added to it, mechanical force would go up in proportion to the energy, while field strength stated 'as volts per metre' would go up in proportion to the square root of energy.

;-----------

An electric field has a force per unit of area (1 meter square area) and it has an energy per unit of volume (1 meter cubed of volume). The two numbers are exactly the same and are calculated by exactly the same equation.

So for example whenever an electric field has a force of 10 Newtons per 1 meter square area, it must also have an energy of 10 Joules per 1 meter cubed of volume!

The formula gave the energy which a radio wave stores in a unit of volume of space. Unit volume was 1 meter cubed . To change the number into the power in Watts per square meter of area, one just multiplies the equation by C the speed of light, which is 300 million meters per second. This is easy to understand since if the radio wave was passing through a window of 1 meter square area, then the volume of it moving through the window every second would be C Meters cube! Which is about 300 million times a 1 meter cube volume.

So the formula which gives Joules energy stored per unit volume of space, simply has to be multiplied times C, and the formula with C is the power of a radio wave in Watts per 1 square metre area.

$$\frac{1}{2}\epsilon_o E^2 C$$

So watts power of electric field alone per 1 square metre area is
Remove the ½ if you include the magnetic field as well.
The electric field and the magnetic field both store an equal amount of energy in a volume of space. So you can imagine that where there is a radio wave you can take a cube shaped volume of empty space, and the total energy in that cube of volume of empty space is half coming from the electric field and half coming from the magnetic field.

I have read that it is the simplest when that volume is unit volume or that is 1 meter cube. I have read that in every case the "force per unit area = energy per unit volume", as both are exactly the

$$\frac{1}{2}\epsilon_o E^2$$

same number, and for the electric field that is equal to   But really the word "unit" is not necessary, since naturally "force per area = energy per volume" and it works with any area and volume. Where the symbol epsilon is the constant called the permittivity of space
$\epsilon_o = 8.854*10^{-12}$ And E is electric field strength in volts per metre
The other half of the energy in an electromagnetic wave is from the magnetic field. For the magnetic field it is also true that "force per area = energy per volume" and that is written in two

$$\frac{1}{2}\mu_o H^2$$

ways, one using the letter B and one using H. Using H it is   where H stands for a magnetic field measured in Amperes per metre. The constant $\mu_o = 4\pi*10^{-7}$ is the permeability of free space.

$$\frac{1}{2}\mu_o H^2 C$$

The power of the magnetic field in a radio wave, per 1 metre square area, must be
watts and always equal to the power of the electric field. Just remove the ½ to get total power. Always in every case force per area is equal to energy per volume, and I think this is because of the concept of mechanical work. The force on the square side of a 1 metre wide cube of empty space

can do a certain amount of mechanical work as it pushes along the depth of that cube, which is in the case of unit volume always a depth of 1 metre. So force on an area of 1 pushing along a depth of 1, gives the energy per unit of volume.

While the force pushes along the whole depth of that cube, the field vanishes as all its power is used up.

 But in the case of the magnetic field the same force per unit area can also be found using the

letter B as Force per 1 meter square = $\frac{1}{2}\frac{B^2}{\mu_o}$

 The magnetic field is measured in these 2 different ways, it is measured either as H = amperes per metre, or it is measured a different way as B which stands for Tesla. I preferred the equation using the letter H, because it looks very similar to the electric field equation. I think it might be better to use H, because you want to remember that in radio waves the electric field part is exactly equal in force to the magnetic field part. The formula written with B does not remind you of that?

The units of measurement for E was volts per metre, and for H it was amperes per metre, and that makes the two fields look different by a factor of 377, but in reality they are both the same strength in any radio wave. (I thought it would be nice if they were measured in units which would show you immediately whenever they are really equal in strength).

To find a magnetic field H exactly equal in strength to an electric field E, you divide E by about 377, because of the equation

$\frac{E}{Z_o} = H$ $Z_o = characteristic-of-impedance-of-vacuum$ $Z_o \ is \approx 120\,\pi$ Or approximately

$Z_o = 377$

So therefore an electric field of 1 volt per metre, is equal in strength to a magnetic field H of

$\frac{1}{377}$ Amperes per metre. Or a magnetic field of H=1 is really equal in strength to an electric field

of about 377 volts per metre. I have also read some other formulas $E = cB$ And $B^2 = \mu_o^2 H^2$ And the two constants are connected with the speed of light, and that the speed of light squared

$C^2 = \frac{1}{[\mu_o \epsilon_o]}$ I also read that $\mu_o C = Z_o$ and $E = \mu_o C H = Z_o H$

But I am going to avoid writing B for a magnetic field and will use H.

The power carried by a radio waves electric field through a 1 meter square area is

$Watts\_per\_square\_metre = \frac{1}{2}\epsilon_o E^2 C$ The total power is exactly twice that when the magnetic field is included, as the magnetic field of a radio wave carries the other half of the power.

And you just add the speed of light = C to the equation that was for "energy per volume" to get the power per area. (as C= 300 million meters per second).

For example the power of a radio wave in watts going through an area measured in square meters was written as $P = \epsilon_o E_{rms}^2 C [Area]$ And actually because the field strengths in a radio wave are changing following a cosine rule as they go past you, E should really be the root-mean-square voltage, E_{rms} to be accurate. And E_{rms}^2 is exactly half of the maximum or peak value of E^2.

Anyway it is easy to imagine that if a radio wave is flying through a window of 1 meter square, (unit area), then every time the radio wave moves forward a distance of 1 metre, a 1 meter cubed volume of it goes through the window.

As it moves at the speed of 300,000,000Meters per second, that many cubic meters of volume of it have passed through the window every second. Therefore the letter C is added to the equation to get the power in watts (Joules per second). The speed of light is about 3 metres every 10 nanoseconds.

So when a window is 1 meter square, and approximately every 3.3 nanosecond a radio wave moves through a distance of 1 metre, a 1 meter cubed volume of the radio wave goes through the window. So you multiply the energy per unit of volume by C, to get the power.

Even with a rather powerful radio wave the energy per volume of space is actually quite small, and it's just that a very large volume of the fields flies through the area every second, the large volume adds up to the total power.

And because in a radio wave the two fields each carry half of the total energy, you can write the total energy per 1 square meter area, which a radio wave passes through just by removing the ½.

Total watts per one square meter of a radio wave = $\epsilon_o E^2 C$ when both electric and magnetic fields are included, but only E is necessary in the equation. Or instead you can write = $\mu_o H^2 C$ which is the same total power.

The total power over an area must be $Watts = \epsilon_o E^2 C [Area]$ if Area is in square metres.

And I have read that actually in a radio wave the field strength that passes by you changes with a cosine rule as the wave goes past you, and so I read E^2 should be the root mean square value of E or E_{rms}^2 to be accurate, as in the waveform peak power is twice the average power .

I have read that the formula for "force per area" of an electric field written as F measured as Volts per metre, can apply equally well to both the electric field in between the wide spaced plates of a parallel plate capacitor, and to the electric field of a radio wave. It is strange, physicists think both the radio wave and the plate capacitor have the same type of electric field, and use the same formula for both when expressing their energy stored in a volume of space.

So the magnetic field of a radio wave is considered to have a force over an area, as well as energy per volume. And it seems clear that they think the force and energy belongs to the field itself, as you don't need to calculate anything about electric charges.

Since the field that ball lightning is made of must be very similar to the half cycle of a radio wave, this all applies to ball lightning. Or at least energy per volume, (which always equals force per area,) and field strength, can apply very well to ball lightning. But the power in watts per area wouldn't apply, as the ball lightning is just moving with its spinning in a small circle.

If you know the energy stored in an electric field, and want to know its strength in Volts per metre,

$$Joules - energy - per - unit - volume = \frac{1}{2}\epsilon_o E^2$$

you can rearrange the formula   to get E.

$$E = \sqrt{2\frac{Joules - per - 1m^3}{8.854 * 10^{-12}}}$$ $$E = 10^6 \sqrt{\frac{Joules - per - 1m^3}{4.427}}$$ and so   So for example, when an

electric field contains energy of 1 Joule per 1 meter cubed volume of space, its field strength in

$$10^6 \frac{1}{\sqrt{4.472}} = \frac{10^6}{2.104} = 475,275 \quad Volts - per - metre$$

volts per meter should be   That is nearly half a million volts over a metre.

$$E, Volts - per - metre = \frac{10^6}{2.104} * \sqrt{Joules - per - 1m^3}$$ In general, when the energy is of an electric

field alone. But when it is a radio wave the magnetic field carries an equal amount of energy as the electric field, so when you use the total energy which is exactly twice that of the electric field,

$$Volts - per - metre = \frac{10^6}{2.9755} * \sqrt{Total - Joules - per - 1m^3}$$

Electric Fields

I have read that the electric field in a radio wave has a force per area and it has an energy per volume of space. I thought it was useful to use that simple formula and make a little table showing the force which the electric field has per area. The input was the electric field E in volts per metre. The output was the force per 1 meter square area, and the energy per 1 meter cube volume. The only formula used to make this table was $\frac{1}{2}\epsilon_o E^2$

Electric field Volts per Meter Volts	Force per 1 square meter in Newtons	Energy per 1 cubic meter, in Joules
1,000	0.00000442	0.00000442
100,000	0.0442	0.0442
1,000,000	4.427	4.427
10,000,000	442.7	442.7
100,000,000	44270	44270

I hope I have not made a mistake in this table, it follows the simple formula, and according to what I have read it should apply equally well to the electric field in between plates of a parallel plate capacitor and to the electric field of a radio wave in space.

In the case of the radio wave in space there are no electric charges to create the field, but it should have the same force measured in Newtons per 1 square meter area and the same energy in Joules which it stores in a 1 meter cube volume of space.

In the radio wave the magnetic field is thought to carry the other half of the total energy, so in the case of a radio wave the total energy per volume should be double the amount in the table.

As you can see, in every example the force per area is the same as the energy stored per volume. And when there is 10 million volts per meter the force per 1 square meter area should be about 442 Newtons which is about 44 kilograms, while energy stored per 1 meter cube of space is about 442 Joules. But with 100 million volts per meter the force on 1 square meter area should be about 4.4 Tonnes.

One worked example for 10 million volts per meter is this. 10 million square is 10^{14} and $\frac{1}{2}\epsilon_o = 4.427 \times 10^{-12}$ so $4.427 \times 10^{-12} \times 10^{14} = 442.7$

As you can see in the table when the electric field is only 1000 Volts per metre, its energy per 1 meter cube volume should be only 0.00000442 Joules. Now when a radio wave has an electric field strength of 1000 volts per metre, you know it is a fairly strong radio wave. But its energy per volume is only double that really small number, (double since there is both an electric part and a magnetic part) and imagine that the radio wave is passing through a window of 1 meter square.

You know that because it is moving forward at 300 million meters per second, the volume of its fields in cubic meters where it passes through the 1 metre square window must be 300 million cubic meters every second.
And 0.00000442 times 300,000,000 is 1326, the power of the electric field in the radio wave in watts (Joules per second) as that passes through the 1 meter square window. Actually this is the power of its electric field alone, and the magnetic field is thought to carry the other half of the energy.
So if this is right, a radio wave of 1326 x2 Watts = 2652 Watts, going through a 1 meter square window, should have a voltage of 1000 volts per meter where it actually gets through the window? This should be a root-mean-square voltage? I am not an expert in this and not quite sure that these figures are right.

I have read a witness said a ball of lightning floated into a barrel of cold water, and the water got hot, which means it had a lot of energy. The energy which heats 1 litre of water by 1 degree C is a K Calorie, which is about 4200 Joules. The table about the energy of an electric field per 1 meter cubed volume of space, might imply that to have so much energy the ball of lightning may have had an electric field strength of about 100 million to 300 million volts per metre?
And the amazing thing is that in general ball lightning with a very strong field power did not cause strong electric currents arcing in the air, while the ball lightning was in the air. A strong electric current would drain away all the energy very very quickly, and obviously it does not happen. A strong electric current would probably make ball lightning explode in the air and vanish in a second, and instead it is stable.

The only explanation I can think of for why the ball lightning does not induce strong electric currents in the air, is that its electric field must be pointing evenly and uniformly outward away from the ball's centre, or in the opposite direction, evenly towards the centre. If the electric field points in a radial direction away from the centre of the ball and has evenly the same strength everywhere, then maybe it won't induce strong electric currents through the air.

A centrifugal force

What should make the super-polarized waves travel in curves and then in circles? One theory of a possibility would be the magnetic field joining their north and south sides? The super-polarized waves, like other half-wavelengths, or half-cycles, have a north side and a south side,. (Since there is no cycle, it's not right to call them half-cycles once they have passed through the filter). Magnetic lines of force could form joining their north side to their south side, and when that happens the field could move a bit more slowly on the side where the slow or motionless magnetic lines of force are joining its upper and lower sides. This could curve its flight path, bending it towards the side where it moves a bit more slowly.

Half the energy of an electromagnetic wave is considered to be carried by an electric field, and half of the energy is thought to be carried by a magnetic field. If you consider the electric field's energy alone, I have read that the energy per 1 cubic meter of volume in space is

$$Joules\,energy = \frac{1}{2}\epsilon_o E^2$$

If it is a unit of volume.

And when there is more than 1 cubic meter of volume, the field's energy must be

$$Joules\,energy = \frac{1}{2}\epsilon_o E^2 [Volume]$$

while E is the electric field strength in volts per metre.

$$Force\,Newtons = \frac{1}{2}\epsilon_o E^2 [Area]$$

And the force of an electric field over an area is . Area is in square metres.

If something moves in a circle, its centripetal acceleration in Meters per second per second, is $\frac{V^2}{R}$

and in this case V is the speed of light C so the centripetal acceleration is $\frac{C^2}{R}$ (and C^2 is 90,000 million million). (Note: Just above here, and often I used the letter E to mean electric field strength, but here the letter E is for energy in Joules. I will write E_j with the small "j" for energy in Joules).

From energy, $E_j = MC^2$ you find the mass which is $M = \frac{E_j}{C^2}$ Centripetal force is mass times acceleration, it would be

$$centripetal\,force = \frac{C^2}{R} \times \frac{E_j}{C^2} = \frac{E_j}{R}$$

So the C^2 above and below the equation cancels out, and you see that the centripetal force which is necessary to keep the ball lightning spinning in a circle depends on just the energy E in Joules and the radius R in metres.

As the speed of light square cancels out, the equation becomes very simple.

$$Centrifugal\,Force_{Newtons} = \frac{Joules\,of\,Energy}{Radius\,in\,meters}$$

Its Centrifugal force is equal to

Of course this formula is specific for ball lightning, and is not for other spinning objects.

Centrifugal and centripetal force are equal and opposite in anything that spins. So it looks like a ball of lightning with an energy of 1 Joule and a radius of 1 meter would have a centrifugal force of 1 Newton.

And so it would need something to cause a 1 Newton centripetal force to keep it spinning in a circle.

If its radius were 0.1 meters, its needed centripetal force would be just 10 times greater, and if its energy was 1 Joule, it would need a centripetal force of 10 Newton to keep it spinning in a circle. And a ball lightning with a stored energy of 10 Joules and with a radius of 0.1Meters would have a centrifugal and centripetal force of 100 Newton.

The following table is so simple, but the centrifugal force caused by the quick spinning is given for a few simple examples of ball size and its stored energy.

Ball Lightning Radius in Metres	Ball Lightning Stored Energy in Joules	Centrifugal Force of Ball Lightning in Newtons
1	1	1
1	10	10
1	10,000	10,000
0.1	1	10
0.1	10	100
0.1	10,000	100,000

The formula for the centrifugal force of ball lightning is so very simple, and you want to do a rough calculation to show whether or not the strength of the field would be enough to overcome the centrifugal force, which means I assume somehow create the centripetal force pointing to the centre, which is equal and opposite to the centrifugal force in any spinning object.

In the above table a ball of lightning with a stored energy of 1 Joule and with a radius of 1 meter should have a centrifugal force of 1 Newton, the centrifugal force caused because it is spinning so quickly.

An interesting thing was how this goes with the two simple formula which calculated force per area, and energy per volume of either an electric field or of a magnetic field.

For example when a field stores an energy of 1 Joule in a 1 meter cube volume of space, then the field must have a force of 1 Newton per 1 meter squared of area. You can see from this that by coincidence the force of a field storing 1 Joule per 1 meter cubed, is just about the same as the 1 Newton of centrifugal force of a ball lightning that has 1 Joule energy. Which shows that the field strength in a ball lightning should be about enough to overcome the centrifugal force which it has because it is spinning.

The force of a field is supposed to be applied over an area in square meters, and I do not know how the forces in a ball lightning are acting to attract toward the centre, but a rough calculation shows that the force acting on an area roughly equal to the area of the sphere shape and pulling roughly towards the centre would be just about strong enough, or maybe 1.5x stronger.
This ratio is not a variable, instead it turns out that it should be a fixed ratio, not affected by energy or by radius.

It is interesting that they say that electric and magnetic fields have a force per area which is always equal to their energy per volume of space. For example, when the energy which an electric field stores in space is 1 Joule per 1 cubic meter of Volume, then the force per area of the field is 1

$$Force = \frac{1}{2} \epsilon_o E^2 [Area]$$

Newton per 1 squared meter of Area. According to the well known formula

And exactly the same is true for a magnetic field. The point of mentioning it is this fits perfectly with the definition that the energy of 1 Joule is made by a movement with the force of 1 Newton over the distance of 1 metre. The amount of energy in a field is the same whether it gets to do work electrically or mechanically. (mechanically the two plates of a parallel plate capacitor will be attracted to each other. If the two plates move closer together, the field between them is used up, and its energy is converted to mechanical energy, in proportion to how much the volume vanishes when the two plates come together. The field between two capacitor plates can give you exactly the same amount of energy either mechanically or electrically. I read in lecture notes that the electric field can be considered to have the energy in its volume of space, and you do not need to think about electric charges, which is good as that simplifies things.)

With a rough calculation that is certainly not accurate, you can see that the force of either the electric field or the magnetic field can be strong enough to overcome the natural centrifugal force which ball lightning has because it spins so quickly.
In a radio wave the energy is spread out over a very large volume of fields, which causes the impression that the field is weak and especially that it has little mechanical force.

It does have a mechanical force with its fields, but an illusion, only an illusion of being mechanically very weak comes from the dilution over a large volume, as the waves are diluted by being spread out. But with the ball lightning the fields would be superimposed on top of one another, adding together. And so ball lightning is a more concentrated field than a radio wave, having more energy concentrated in a small volume. Therefore there would not be the false impression of it not having much mechanical force, on the contrary an artificially made ball lightning could probably explode with an obvious mechanical force sometimes.

Interesting and Exciting Experiments one might try with Ball Lightning

Once you have made super-polarized waves, you should be 99% of the way towards creating ball lightning.!

From then on creating the ball lightning should be quite simple. You would just have to hang in the air a small piece of magnetized iron wire or a tiny magnet. Or a little ball with an electrostatic charge could be tried instead of a magnet. You could tie the small piece of magnetized iron wire to the end of a thread, and tie the other end of the thread to a long bamboo pole.

And then just hang the small piece of magnetized iron so that it is turned around the right way: It's North end should be a bit closer to the South side of the beam of super-polarized waves, and its South end should be a bit closer to the magnetic North side of the beam of super-polarized waves, so that you would normally expect them to be attracted.

Immediately ball lightning should form in the air around the little piece of iron wire, and ball lightning might also form in other places where you don't expect it.

The process could start when the small piece of iron wire is hanging in the air. First the flight path of some of the field would be curved toward the piece of iron wire.

Then some of the energy in the field of the super-polarized waves would spin around the short piece of iron wire in circles of rapidly diminishing size, and very quickly ball lightning would form in the air around the iron wire. This ball lightning would be identical in every way to the natural thing, but it would be caught onto the piece of iron wire which would stay at it's centre.

While the equipment is turned on, more and more energy of the super-polarized waves would join the ball lightning and so it would be charged up with more and more power. The ball lightning would continue to get more and more energy until something causes a limit to its energy. For example friction might form a limit and also it might burn up the thread and the thing might fall onto the floor.

But if you turned off the equipment the ball lightning should exist for a few minutes on its own and I suppose that is true since natural ball lightning does sometimes last a few minutes.

When the ball lightning disappears after a few minutes it might still be there really, but transparent and invisible because its power is lower.

You could not stand in the beam of super-polarized waves since the beam would probably give you strong electric shocks. So the beam of super-polarized waves might be deadly, and you would have to stand back safely and you would need a long pole to be able to reach into the beam.

So you would need a long bamboo pole or a fishing rod, tie a thread to the end of the long pole, and tie to the other end of the thread to your small magnet or a piece of iron wire, or a plastic ball with an electrostatic charge. And use the long pole to reach into the beam of super-polarized half-cycles.

And ball lightning should form in the air around the small piece of iron, immediately.

But as well as making ball lightning in the air around a small slightly magnetized object, there should be a way to get the ball lightning to form so that it floats completely free in the air, by itself rather than form around a small magnet or a piece of iron wire.

The strong beam of super-polarized waves would be awfully interesting to experiment with. Small obstacles such as small pieces of plastic with the right shapes should probably trigger ball lightning to form in the air floating completely free and you need to experiment to find what shapes can trigger that formation of ball lightning in the air, as you place the objects in different positions within the beam of super-polarized waves.

Imagine that you were random experimenting. Then sometimes the ball lightning would be caught around a small object it holds at its centre, and sometime the ball lightning would float free in the air by itself.

One might compare the spinning to the fact that whenever there is a wind in the air and the wind flies around an obstacle, that causes little spinning currents or eddies in the air.

If you have made a strong beam of super-polarized waves, ball lightning might also form in other places where you don't expect it. As for example ball lightning would form around steel screws inside wooden tables, and ball lightning might form quickly around non-magnetic objects when they have a normal electrostatic charge.

Of course when the small objects are hanging to the right hand side of the beam of super-polarized waves that would produce clockwise spinning ball lightning, but when they are hanging to the left hand side of the beam that would produce counter-clockwise spinning ball lightning.

If a part of its spinning field starts to fly away in other directions because it is being deflected or because you have moved a piece of metal into it, this would make a bang of a strong explosion.

If you use two bamboo poles with a thread tied to the end of each pole, then you could try an experiment to make an explosion. Firstly assuming that you have a strong beam of super-polarized waves, make ball lightning form in the air around one small piece of magnetized iron wire, and then move it away from the beam of super-polarized waves.

Taking a second bamboo pole, and a second piece of magnetized iron wire hanging from its end with a thread, you can create a second ball of lightning to find out what happens when two of them meet. Or simply use a plain piece of iron wire. Switch off the power, and gradually turn the bamboo poles so that the second piece of iron wire, or a second ball of lightning comes very close to the first.

When the other piece of iron wire comes too close to the ball lightning and touches it, the spinning ball might well explode with a very loud bang, and in that explosion several new balls of lightning could form, and some of these might go floating completely free in the air.

Some of the new balls of lightning formed in the explosion might shoot through the air very quickly.

They might well fly through the air at thousands of miles per hour. It would be a good idea to have a wire mesh screen in front of you to avoid being hit by it. The balls of lightning will have a strong force per area in Newtons probably equal to their energy per volume in Joules. For example an energy of 1,000 Joules per 1 metre cubed of its volume, would probably mean the ball has a force of 1,000 Newtons per 1 square metre of its surface area.

If you consider their strong force acting over an area, it is obvious that disrupting one could make a loud bang. It is simply a question of some of the energy that was spinning in circles, flying apart in another direction for a short distance and for a moment.

I wonder, what exactly would cause the ball lightning to contract into a round spinning ball when it's on its own in the air? I don't know. There is a magnetic field, and super-polarized waves have a North side and a South side which is a simple natural consequence of the fields in all radio waves having a magnetic field vector.

In normal radio waves these fields alternate in opposite directions, so any external field which might form to join their sides will be immediately cancelled out.

The cancelling out would not happen with super-polarized waves because they all point the same way. A lack of cancelling out will reveal things not seen with radio waves, but natural for some electromagnetic fields. Radio waves are never deflected by motionless electric or magnetic fields. Not in the slightest bit, of course. But super-polarized waves can surely be deflected by even motionless electric or magnetic fields.

When super-polarized waves pass by with their north and south sides pointing in the same direction every time, this may let magnetic fields form outside them or around them gradually. Magnetic fields forming around the sides of super-polarized waves might bend them, curve them to make them go in naturally decreasing spirals or circles? If they bend in circles the same magnetic field which caused that might be strengthened by it? But that does not completely explain how it would form a round ball when it is free by itself in the air.

Any new principles would be normal for electromagnetic fields, but, would be things that are cancelled out within radio waves specifically because of the alternating character of radio waves, as they have fields normally called half-cycles which alternate by pointing in two opposite directions. As they come one after another pointing in opposite directions, effects must get cancelled out and vanish before a physicist would ever be able to see them.

Obviously with the fields of ordinary radio waves coming and pointing in opposite directions, two opposite directions, something can be cancelled out. In the special case of all the fields pointing in the same direction, unknown things are not cancelled out naturally. I suppose that physicists do not know all the properties of electromagnetic fields correctly, because they have missed effects that get cancelled out whenever the fields are alternating and point in opposite directions.

Anyway if you have made a strong beam of super-polarized waves, it is possible that natural balls of lightning which float free in the air might form in different places, and minor obstacles a sheet of metal or like bits of metal or even plastic things might trigger the ball lightning to form in the beam of super-polarized waves.

It's as when you have a wind in the air, you often get eddies as spinning whirlpools in the air. And obstacles in the path of the flow of air often cause the little areas of spinning air.

Possibly little obstacles in a beam of super-polarized waves can trigger ball lightning to form immediately, which would sometimes float freely by itself, but which would also sometimes be stuck to small objects, or clinging to something like a screw or a nail which stays held at the centre. And once you have made lots of the ball lightning you could do experiments and measurements and try to find out the answer to these questions.

It is easy to realise that the super-polarized waves would always have naturally a magnetic north side and a magnetic south side which you can suppose would be attracted or repelled depending on direction of a small magnet.

A ball lightning is only a field of forces and does not contain electric currents. To prove it, you could use your long pole to lower a ball lightning into a large tank of oil, or into a large block of solid glass. A large block of solid plastic could have a small diameter hole drilled half way through it, on the top. The round hole would be just large enough for the piece of magnetized iron wire to go into it easily half way through the block.

When you have formed the ball lightning around the piece of iron wire, you would see it glowing and spinning, and you could lower the ball lightning into the solid block of glass, and pull it out again. And probably this could prove that the ball lightning does not need to have an electric current, since glass is an electrical insulator.

Which would prove that there are no electric currents in ball lightning since glass is an insulator. Still I wonder whether the ball lightning not being perfectly balanced as it spins, might transfer some energy as heat to the glass?

Usually and naturally ball lightning is probably a bit lopsided.

Spinning at exactly the speed of light, if it is not exactly balanced and symmetrical it will have some vibrations and so it could lose some energy to the glass? How many seconds or minutes could ball lightning exist inside a block of solid glass or plastic?

You would feel some tugging pulling on the thread when you try to lift the ball lightning back out of the block of glass, because the ball lightning would be a little attracted towards the glass or even strongly attracted to it, because of its refractive index, or rather its dielectric effects.

;-------------------

If you have a strong beam of the super-polarized waves and a tiny bar magnet is placed to one side of the beam, a ball of lightning should be created immediately in the air around it. It needs space so it would be best to hang it from the end of a long thread. You could not stand in the beam of super-polarized waves, because of the danger of getting a very strong electric shock which might be deadly.

Possibly super-polarized waves would give you much worse electric shocks than radio waves which have the same power and the same measured volts per meter, because perhaps in the human body electric currents are carried by ions?

So you need a long fishing rod or a bamboo pole with a thread tied to its end, so you can reach forward into the beam safely. Definitely the super-polarized waves could give severe electric shocks continually, so you couldn't stand near it. Depending on whether you hang the small piece of iron wire to the right side of the beam of super-polarized half cycles, or to the left side of the beam, you would get ball lightning which spins either clockwise or anti-clockwise in a simple way.

An obvious idea is that a ball lightning which is floating free in the air should have a tiny amount of mass according to $E = MC^2$. I said the ball lightning can be either floating freely in the air or it can be attached to a small magnet or a piece of magnetized iron wire held by a thread in the air. It can probably also be held by a small electro-statically charged ball which you could hang from the end of the thread instead of a magnet. But there can easily be an explosion with a loud bang, which would happen when you move a second piece of magnetized iron into or too close to the ball lightning.

And another easy to do experiment, would be to see if the direction of spinning of two balls of lightning affects the force of the explosion when the two meet? Bring together two balls of lightning and see whether they explode sooner or with a louder bang if they were spinning in opposite directions?

 And in every such an explosion some of the energy could be suddenly converted into radio waves, plus often the energy would go into creating secondary balls of lightning which would often be floating completely free in the air. They might shoot across the room quickly.

 In any such explosion what could happen much too quickly to see is that some of the super-polarized fields which were spinning around in a small circle would for a moment stop spinning, and fly outward nearly in straight lines, in a different direction. And if they fly apart in nearly straight lines suddenly, they could very often start spinning in circles again a bit further away. That would form new balls of lightning in the air nearby.

;----------------------

 An amount of momentum means that centripetal acceleration requires a centripetal force, even when something moving in a circle is in some way mass-less. As anything spins in a circle there has to be a centripetal acceleration always pointing to the exact centre of the circle, and the tiny momentum of the field means that a centripetal force exists even if it is considered mass-less.

It turns out that the centripetal acceleration is quite strong as it has to be proportional to the square of the speed. And so it has to be proportional to the square of the speed of light, which
$C^2 = 90,000 \, million \, million$

And it was interesting to try to guess the approximate magnetic field strength and show that it could be strong enough to create the necessary centripetal force and overcome the tendency to fly apart which is called centrifugal force.

The formula for field strength does not involve frequency.

A formula which connects field strength in Volts per meter to the power W in Watts per square metre, was: $W = c \epsilon_o E_v^2$, where W is power in Watts, C is the speed of light in meters per second, and the epsilon is the constant called permittivity of space. $= 8.854 \times 10^{-12}$ and E_v is the electric field strength in Volts per metre.

The formula for the Energy per unit volume of an electromagnetic wave was the same except without the C. That is $E = \epsilon_o E_v^2$ for energy in Joules per unit volume, and the unit volume is 1 meter cube. Because if you imagine a radio wave going through a window of 1 meter square area, then as it moves 300 million meters a second the volume that goes through the window every second must be 300 million meters cubed. And therefore the letter C is added to the equation to get the power in watts.

The assumed mass of the ball lightning depends on its energy, and $E = MC^2$ so mass $M = \dfrac{E}{C^2}$

;--------------------

The ball-lighting must have a very tiny amount of mass according to Einstein's famous equation: $E=MC^2$

Where E the energy can be in Joules, M is kilograms mass, and C is the speed of light as 300,000,000 Meters per second. A Joule is the energy of 1 watt for 1 second. Also 1 Joule is exactly the same thing as a force of 1 Newton pushing something through a distance of 1 metre. And a force of 1 Newton is the force which can give a mass of 1 kilogram an acceleration of 1 meter per second per second.

The mass of the ball-lighting is then $M = \dfrac{E}{C^2}$ where C^2 is the speed of light squared.

And the speed of light squared is 90,000 million million, or $90 x 10^{15}$

Supposing a weak ball lightning has only 1 Joule of energy stored in it, it would probably be invisible as that amount of energy is so low, perhaps too low to be visible, and its mass would be $\dfrac{1}{C^2}$ kilograms, or approximately 1/(90 million) micrograms, which is $\dfrac{1}{90,000}$ nano-grams. (The nano-gram is a billionth of a gram).

Supposing a ball lightning had an energy of 90,000 Joules, then its mass would be 10^{-12} Kilograms.

Which is 1 nano-gram.

If the mass is 1 nano-gram, and the ball of lightning is spinning at the speed of light, it is interesting to find approximately its centrifugal force and its angular momentum.

In general it is interesting that any object which is moving in a circle is accelerating towards the centre of the circle, and to keep an object moving in a circle you only need a force which always points towards the centre of the circle. This force is called a centripetal force, equal in strength to the centrifugal force which is a tendency to fly outwards. When anything is moving in a circle, its

acceleration towards the centre of the circle is always simply: $\dfrac{V^2}{R}$ where V is the speed inMeters per second, and R is the radius of the circle in metres.

The centrifugal force is $\dfrac{MV^2}{R}$ and in this case that is $\dfrac{MC^2}{R}$ which is

$$centrifugal\_force\_newton = \frac{(mass\_kilograms)x(90,000\_million\_million)}{Radius\_metres}$$

And 1 nano-gram is $10^{-12}Kg$

$$Newtons = \frac{(1\_nanogram\_)x(90,000\_million\_million)}{R}$$

Or $\dfrac{10^{-12}\_x90\_x10^{15}}{R}$ $=$ $\dfrac{9x10^4}{R}$ Newtons force. And R is the radius of the ball of lightning. If the ball was 2Meters in diameter, R=1, so this is about 90,000 Newton, or about 9000 Kilograms of force. When something spins that quickly 1 nanogram of mass can produce a centrifugal force of 9 tonnes!

This seems to be a strange result, and it is interesting to find the approximate field strength of a ball lightning which stores in its field different examples of energy levels, to see whether the field strength would be enough to hold it in a ball shape against the centrifugal force which tries to make the ball fly apart and break up.

 It turned out according to a certain calculation about ball lightning of much lower and several different energy levels, that either the electric field strength considered alone, or the magnetic field strength considered alone, had about 1.5 times the force which might be necessary to balance centrifugal force and keep it from expanding outwards.

The centrifugal force is as you can see inversely proportional to the radius R, and if the ball lightning was a lot smaller or maybe 20 cm in diameter making its radius =0.1 meters,   the centrifugal force would get 10 times greater. (as one divides by 0.1). A smaller radius R means a greater acceleration.

The centrifugal force is simply and directly proportional to the mass of the ball lightning over its radius, while its mass is simply and directly proportional to its energy.

So if you assume a ball lightning of 2Meters diameter and with 90K Joules energy has a centrifugal force of approximately 90,000 Newton then a ball lightning of merely 90 Joules energy would have to have a centrifugal force of about 90 Newton force, and if its energy was 10 Joules its centrifugal force should be about 10 Newton, and if its energy were 1 Joule only, the centrifugal force would be about 1 Newton force. (which is about 100 grams force). A ball lightning with 1 Joule total energy and 0.1 meter radius should have a centrifugal force of about 10 Newton, or about 1 Kg force

I wanted to try to work out an approximate value for its field strength in volts per metre, or its natural magnetic field in Amperes per metre, to see whether it is possible for its normal magnetic field to be strong enough attraction to keep the whole field moving in a circle, and I will do that further on.

The mass of the ball lightning depends on $\dfrac{1}{C^2}$ and so is extremely tiny, whereas the centrifugal force depends on C^2 above the line, or $\dfrac{C^2}{1}$ which is a very large number. And so because the speed of light squared is a very large number even a very tiny mass spinning in circles at that speed needs a lot of force to hold it in a circle, as it has quite a strong centripetal acceleration. The centripetal acceleration is not affected by the amount of mass in any way, but is $\dfrac{V^2}{R}$, and it is measured in meters per second per second. When the radius is 1 metre, the acceleration towards the centre of the circle is $\dfrac{C^2}{1}$ which is 90,000 million million Meters per second per second. Which is about 9,000 million million G's of acceleration, and that enormous acceleration has to be towards the centre of the circle and has to be there to keep the tiny mass of the field moving in the circle and to prevent it from flying outwards. So obviously an extremely tiny mass tries to fly outwards and that needs to be countered with a strong enough force. Any mass would feel approximately 9000 million million times its own weight, if it is spinning in a 1 meter radius circle at the speed of light.

What about its angular momentum? I think the angular momentum is a very very much smaller number than the centrifugal force, because it is increased by the simple speed of light whereas centrifugal force is increased by the square of the speed of light..

The angular momentum of any particle around an axis of rotation, is MVR, where MV is the normal linear momentum equal to mass times velocity, and R is the perpendicular distance from the velocity vector V to the axis of rotation. (The distance R to the centre of rotation is at right angles to the velocity vector V). (I think the radius R gives the momentum MV some leverage like the arm of a lever, so longer R increases turning forces.) V can be the velocity of anything on the rim of the circle while radius R is at right angles to that velocity.

Because the angular momentum of a ball lightning depends on the plain speed of light, rather than depending on the square of it, the angular momentum should be very tiny and small by comparison to the centrifugal force.

For example, suppose the ball lightning had a stored energy of 90 Joules and was 2 meters in diameter, which makes the radius R=1. Then you know from the amount of energy which was 90

Joules that its mass would be 0.001 nano-grams, which is $10^{-15} Kilograms$. And its angular momentum would be as normal mass times velocity times radius.

$mass \times velocity \times radius = 300,000,000 \times 10^{-15} = 3 \times 10^{-7}$ An angular momentum equivalent to an extremely light bubble weighing 0.1 milligrams and rotating so its surface moved at 3Meters per second. Anyway, the angular momentum would be tiny, but it would be large by comparison to the extremely tiny microscopic amount of mass. But the angular momentum would be terribly small, almost too tiny to detect by comparison to any normal ordinary solid object.

So I think that if a ball lightning is attached to a piece of magnetized iron wire, you could not see any gyroscopic effects, because they would be so weak compared to the weight of the solid piece of iron wire attached to it. But when a ball lightning is freely floating in the air you might detect gyroscopic effects and it would be observable because as it is free floating the mass is so extremely tiny. Apparently the angular momentum in a spinning ball lightning is very weak, while its centrifugal force is very strong.

;----------

A ratio of field strength to centrifugal force.

Both the field strength of ball lightning and its centrifugal force would depend on how much energy it has, and I wanted to find very roughly what the field strength would be for a particular value of centrifugal force, to try to see whether the magnetic field strength would be strong enough to counter the tendency of the ball lightning to fly outwards as it spins.
That is I wondered, can the magnetic field strength be as strong as the force you need to prevent the spinning field from flying apart? The result of having tried to do that calculation was that it could be approximately up to 1.5 times strong enough, and that figure would be the same for any size and any energy of ball lightning.

I assumed that in ball lightning the proportions of energy to field strength are approximately the same as they are with radio waves. I have found on the internet some formula which connect the stored energy inside an electromagnetic field to the strength of the field.
I have read that in every case a field's energy per volume is equal to the field's force per area.

The total energy per unit volume of both the electric and the magnetic field in a radio wave is connected to the radio waves' electric field strength in volts per meter by the equation: $W = \varepsilon_o E^2$
This equation connects energy stored in an electromagnetic field of volume 1 meter cubed to its electric field strength in volts per metre. It must apply as well to the super-polarized waves which natural ball lightning is mainly made from. (The constant ε_o is equal to $8.854 x 10^{-12}$)

In any such electromagnetic field moving at the speed of light, the magnetic field strength is exactly equal to the electric field strength. But because a different measurement is used to measure it, the number for volts per meter has to be divided by Z_o which is approximately the number 377, to get the magnetic field strength in H=amperes per metre.

Now that you have the connection between energy stored in the electromagnetic field, and its field strength either in volts per meter or in amperes per metre, the next step is to find the equation for force per area which the field could have. Force per unit area multiplied by an approximate area would give you the total force, and that can be compared to the calculated centrifugal force to find out if that field's force is as strong as the centrifugal force.

I found an equation for the electric field's force per area, and it is $\dfrac{Force}{Area} = \dfrac{1}{2}\varepsilon_o E^2$. Where E is electric field measured as volts per metre. And force per area is in Newtons per square meter. So this connects electric field strength in volts per meter with a force in Newtons, and you see force is proportional to the square of the electric field strength. Just as energy is also proportional to the square of the field strength.

I also found an equivalent equation for the force per area caused by a magnetic field. It gives almost the same result, as it should. The force in Newtons. $\frac{Force}{Area} = \frac{1}{2}\mu_o H^2$. In which H is magnetic field as amperes per metre, and the constant μ_o is $\mu_o = 4\pi 10^{-7}$. Using either equation to connect field strength to force per area, gives the same result.

But what area should you assume the force is acting on, as the greater the area the greater the force?

The ball lightning is almost a sphere, and I used the idea the force of the field would be working on the surface area of that sphere, though assuming that is not exactly right. Obviously this is not intended to be an accurate calculation but something very rough.

If the ball lightning has radius R meters, the surface area of the sphere is $4\pi R^2$, and I find that if the force of the field were acting on the entire surface area of that sphere, then I find it would have 1.5 times the strength of the centrifugal force!

And this ratio of 1.5 seems to be a constant which is not affected by size or by energy.

Of course the field is not acting on the whole area of the sphere, but still the calculation proves that it is possible for the field to have an attracting force which might be strong enough to overcome the centrifugal force which it has because it is spinning at the speed of light.

I show now the worked example of using either the electric field equation. (The magnetic one is similar).

Both force per unit area and energy per unit volume of an electric field are

$$\frac{Force}{Area} = \frac{Energy}{Volume} = \frac{1}{2}\varepsilon_o E^2$$

Where E is Volts per meter. If the radius of the sphere was R meters,

then its volume is $\frac{4}{3}\pi R^3$ Its energy is its energy per volume times the volume, that would be

$$\frac{1}{2}\varepsilon_o E^2 \frac{4}{3}\pi R^3 = Joules\ energy$$

which is for the electric field on its own. The total energy includes the magnetic field and is therefore exactly twice that.

The force per area times the area, is, assuming the area is of a sphere with radius R,

$$\frac{1}{2}\varepsilon_o E^2 \times 4\pi R^2$$

which is $\varepsilon_o E^2 \times 2\pi R^2$ total force possible for an electric field acting on the whole area.

The calculation for centrifugal force was very simple for ball lightning, it is

$$Centrifugal\ Force_{Newtons} = \frac{Joules\ Energy}{Radius}$$

If Joules is the total energy half of which comes from the electric and half from the magnetic fields. It is simple because the C^2 cancelled out above and below the fraction.

Writing $\dfrac{Joules}{radius}$ as $\dfrac{1}{2}\varepsilon_o E^2 \dfrac{4}{3}\pi R^3 x \dfrac{2}{R}$ which is $\varepsilon_o E^2 \dfrac{4}{3}\pi R^2$ So the ratio of possible electric field

$$\dfrac{\varepsilon_o E^2 x 2\pi R^2}{\varepsilon_o E^2 \dfrac{4}{3}\pi R^2} = \dfrac{6}{4}=1.5$$

force over the whole area, divided by the centrifugal force, is:
 So it seems that the ratio of field force per centrifugal force is a constant which is not affected by energy or by radius of the ball lightning. And this constant is roughly near 1.5. A bit lower down I tried the same calculation done assuming that it is the magnetic field which has the force, and it gets exactly the same result of 1.5. A Ball of lightning having any size and any energy level at all would have the same constant ratio, which seems to be an interesting discovery!

The assumptions made were not correct, in reality I suppose that if you knew how to calculate the ratio more accurately, it might perhaps become approximately a 1 to 1 ratio rather than 1.5?

;--------------
And it was already calculated that its centrifugal force is simply

$$centrifugal\ force_{newtons} = \dfrac{Energy_{joules}}{Radius_{metres}}$$

, So the force which the field could have if it acted on the whole area of a sphere is always 1.5 x the centrifugal force. Of course this calculation is not intended to be accurate, since the forces which hold the ball lightning together against the tendency to fly apart which it has because it is spinning, must be mainly a magnetic field which would not be acting on the whole surface of a sphere, but which would act in some other way on a smaller area somewhere.

It must be right to assume that in the field of super-polarized waves, the electric field and the magnetic field must have equal strengths, as the strength of the two fields is equal in any radio wave and it seems to be believed that a leap-frog effect of each field inducing the other one at the speed of light makes them equal.

 But in the ball lightning it may be a magnetic field which has an attractive force which holds it together.
It is obviously not correct to assume that the field is working over the whole surface of a sphere, but if it did work over the surface of the sphere, it would be 1.5 times stronger as the centrifugal force.

 I tried the same calculation with the magnetic field equation instead of the electric field one. It makes exactly the same result.

I have looked for information on the field strength of radio waves and how it depends on the radio waves' power per area. I don't know how to check whether the information I found on the websites was right or not, as this is a subject I don't know much about.

I read that around any radio transmitting antenna there is a near field and a far field. The far field is the radio wave moving away at the speed of light. The near field is mainly other fields which stay close to the antenna. When doing an experiment the special one-way window in the experiments must be in the far field, so it needs to be placed at a distance of at least 1 or 2 wavelengths away from the transmitting antenna, so as to be in the far field.

I found a calculator on a website which is interesting because it lets you calculate the field strength of radio waves in volts per meter at different distances or different power levels. Using it you can see that when a radio wave is 10 times further away from the transmitter, the field strength in volts per meter is just 10 times less, though the power is 100 times less.

 And that must be because the energy in a radio wave is proportional to the square of the electric field strength. Energy is also proportional to the square of the magnetic field strength.

Some examples were power 1 watt/square meter with 19.42 volts/metre and a magnetic field strength of H=0.0515 Amperes/metre.
And another example is 100 watts/square meter with 194.2 Volts/metre, and H=0.515 Amps/metre. This connects power per area with field strength. [In any radio wave, the electric field is always exactly equal strength to the magnetic field, and it only looked different on paper because different units of measurement are used. I assume that when super-polarized half cycles are made from radio waves, then at least at first electric field and magnetic field will have exactly equal strengths, exactly as they do in a radio wave.]

To find the energy per unit volume stored in an electromagnetic wave, and the unit volume is 1 meter cubed, you have to divide the power per unit area by 300 million. Because the radio wave is moving at 300 million meters per second, so that the power per square meter area is stretched out over 300 million metres. And in fact you can take the power per unit area (watts per 1 square metre) and just divide it by 300 million to find the energy in Joules per 1 cubic meter of volume. Half the energy is considered to be stored in its electric field, and half the energy in its magnetic field.

For example, when the power is 1 watt/square metre, the energy per 1 meter cubed must be $\frac{1}{300 million}$ Joules. That energy per 1 meter cubed goes with 19.42 volts/metre field strength.

And for example, when the power was 100 watts/square metre, the energy per 1 meter cubed, must be $\frac{1}{3 million}$ Joules. That must be 0.33 micro joules, which is not much. That went with the

field strength of 194.2 volts/metre.
And the value which I found that way was about the same as the value which you get from an equation which I found on an educational website.

The equation which gave the same result was P= power per unit area carried by an electromagnetic wave. $P = \epsilon_o E^2 c$ In which ϵ_o is the constant 8.854×10^{-12} and E is the electric field strength of the electromagnetic wave in volts per metre, and c is the speed of light in meters per second, or about 300 million.
It also said P was "energy transported per unit time across a unit area perpendicular to the direction in which the wave is travelling".
This connects a radio waves' field strength with power. There was also the equation for energy per unit volume in an electromagnetic wave. The letter U was sometimes used for Energy per unit volume in Joules $U = \epsilon_o E_v^2$ This is the same equation but without the c. The energy per unit volume was for 1 meter cubed. And so energy per unit volume was always 300 million times less than power per unit area. Half the energy is considered to be carried by an electric field, and the other half of the energy by a magnetic field.

The energy per volume of the electric field alone should be in Joules
$$Joules = \frac{1}{2} \epsilon_o E_v^2 [Volume]$$
,
and it's interesting that the same equation is also as well used to find the force of the electric field on an area in Newtons. A unit area, is an area of 1 meter squared. The force of the electric field in Newtons on any larger area is
$$Newtons = \frac{1}{2} \epsilon_o E_v^2 [Area]$$
. I read that the same equation is used both for the electric field part of an electromagnetic wave and for the electric field between the two plates of a parallel plate capacitor. A good thing about this equation is that when you use it you don't specify any electric charges. You can think of both force per area and energy per volume as something that belongs to the field itself without having to think of any electric charges.
You specify only the field strength E in volts per metre, and these formula should give you both the force per area and the energy per volume, which are always two equal numbers.

I think you can assume that values of field strength per energy for radio waves might be very similar to amounts of field strength per energy for ball lightning. To find approximate field strength for a certain amount of energy per unit volume U, the same equation rearranged is:
$$E_v = \frac{\sqrt{U}}{\sqrt{8.854 \times 10^{-12}}} \qquad E_v = 10^6 \frac{\sqrt{U}}{2.975}$$

What I wanted was to approximately relate field strength to energy so as to be able to guess whether the field strength would be enough to overcome the centrifugal force caused by the field spinning so quickly. The centripetal acceleration of anything moving in a circle with radius R, is

$\dfrac{V^2}{R}$ which in this case is $\dfrac{C^2}{R}$. C was the speed of light and R could be 1 meter radius when the ball lightning is 2Meters in diameter. Can the field strength hold the spinning field so that it spins in a circle rather than flying outward?

Notice that in a radio wave the magnetic field strength is always actually equal to the electric field strength, but you don't see it because of the way different units of measurements are used, like E and H. So an electric field of E=194 volts per meter is actually equal strength to a magnetic field of H=0.515 Amperes/metre, even though it looks different. (You divide E by the constant Z_o which is approx 377 to get H, when actually in reality E and H were equal.) And as the 194 volts per meter is really equal strength to magnetic field of 0.515 amperes per metre, they can both produce equal forces per area in Newtons.

1 Joule is the energy of 1 watt for 1 second. Now as the radio wave travels 300,000 kilometres per second the energy per unit volume of the radio wave in a place near to the antenna where you have measured its power, is equal to its power in watts divided by that distance of 300,000,000 metres. It has gone that distance in 1 second so its power watts per square meter measured in that place, has to be divided by the volume of that field as it passes by you for 1 second, (volume in metres cubed.) So the energy in 1 second has to be divided by that distance to get its energy per one meter cubed of volume.

So in the case when its power is 100 watts per square metre, its energy per 1 meter cubed is 100/300,000,000 Joules per cubic metre. This is about 0.333×10^{-6} joules per 1 meter cubed. If its wavelength happens to be 2 meters, then this is about the energy in 1 of its half-cycles. If the transmitter power was 10,000 watts, then the energy in 1 half cycle would be $3,33 \times 10^{-5}$ Joules. You see that to get a radio wave in which 1 half cycle contains just 1 joule energy, the power would need to be 300 megawatts, which is not practical.

When you have produced a beam of super-polarized half cycles, they do not really need to have very much energy individually because the ball lightning is going to get charged up as more and more super-polarized waves being added to it and joining it. I mean it would be normal for the growing ball lightning to get more and more power as fields added to it from the super-polarized waves which come along and get added to it.

;--------

A calculation of ball lightning centrifugal force

So the calculation which I had thought of was not intended to be very accurate, but it is to try to approximately find the field strength associated with a certain amount of centrifugal force. To see if the field strength seems to be sufficient to overcome the centrifugal force which tries to make the spinning ball fly apart.

For any object spinning in circles, the centripetal acceleration is $\dfrac{V^2}{R}$ and in this case it probably goes at exactly the speed of light, so the centripetal acceleration is $\dfrac{C^2}{R}$. Now this is not very accurate because it assumes that all the spinning ball lightning has one radius R, whereas in fact inner parts of it would probably do more turns per second and would turn in a smaller radius. And that would mean that the average centrifugal force would be a bit stronger than according to the non-accurate assumption that it all turns with one radius.

The centrifugal force is usually defined as a tendency to fly apart because things want to travel in straight lines, and the centrifugal force equals the centripetal force but is in the opposite direction. The centripetal force is a real force which points towards the centre of a circle whenever something is moving in a circle, and it is mass times acceleration.

You know $E=MC^2$ and so the mass of ball lightning is $M=\dfrac{E_j}{C^2}$ in which M is the ball lightning's mass in kilograms, and E_j is the ball lightning's total energy in Joules, and C^2 is the speed of light squared in metres per second. So as centripetal force is Mass x Acceleration, and as the acceleration of anything moving in a circle is simply $acceleration=\dfrac{V^2}{R}$ the centripetal force is approximately $\dfrac{E_j}{C^2}\times\dfrac{C^2}{R}$, and the speed of light squared above and below the fraction cancels out so $centrifugal\ force=\dfrac{Energy}{Radius}$ in the case of ball lightning.

When anything spins in a circle the centripetal force is mass times acceleration while acceleration is towards the centre. In this case, the equation for the Mass of the ball lightning has the square of the speed of light below the line as $\dfrac{E_j}{C^2}$, and the centripetal acceleration of the ball lightning as it spins in its circle has the square of the speed of light above the dividing line, as $\dfrac{C^2}{R}$ so the square of the speed of light cancels out. And the result is that the centrifugal force of ball lightning is just $\dfrac{E_j}{R}$ without having the speed of light in it as it cancelled out.

As the C^2 cancels out above and below the fraction, the centrifugal force and the centripetal force which both have to be equal are calculated as just the total energy in Joules divided by the radius in metres. Of course this equation is specific to ball lightning, though the centripetal acceleration formula applies to everything that is spinning in a circle.

I thought it is interesting to try to figure out what the force of the ball lightning field would be to compare that force with the centrifugal force and find out whether it is strong enough? Either the electric field or the magnetic field has a force per area. And the force per area is proportional to the square of the field strength, which makes the force per area proportional to the energy.

I assume that the force per area of either the magnetic or the electric field is the same as it would be in a radio wave. (If it had the same volts per metre strength.) (And you have the formula for force per unit area which is always the same number as energy per unit volume.)
Obviously the force per area, has an effect over an area which is multiplied by the amount of area, so the force can depend on the area measured in square metres. To calculate this roughly I assumed that the area which the force acts on is the surface of a sphere, and that assumption is

$$Force = \frac{1}{2} \epsilon_o E^2 [Area]$$

not at all accurate. For an electric field,   And for a magnetic field,

$$Force = \frac{1}{2} \mu_o H^2 [Area]$$

And you can imagine that the area could be the surface of a sphere with the same diameter as a ball of lighting.

The answer is that the ball lightning field is strong enough, and though I don't understand what holds it together, its magnetic field or its electric field, either of them alone, is strong enough.

I assume that like radio waves, the electric field and the magnetic field each share half of the total energy. Assuming that the connection between field strength and energy per volume is approximately the same as it is for radio waves.

The ratio of field force to centrifugal force, this time for the magnetic field.
The ratio of fields force to centrifugal force turns out to be a fixed constant ratio. Firstly with ball lightning

$$Centrifugal_{force_{newtons}} = \frac{Total_{energy_{Joules}}}{Radius_{Metres}}$$

(With a radio wave half the total energy is stored in the electric field and half of the energy is stored in the magnetic field. I am assuming that super-polarized waves are the same.)

$$\frac{1}{2} \mu_o H^2 A = magnetic\ force\ in\ Newtons$$

I had found a formula for magnetic force per area.   , where
A = Area in square meters,   and H = magnetic field in amperes per metre.

It is very similar to the formula for an electric field's attraction force in Newton per area, which was

$$\frac{1}{2}\epsilon_o E^2 A = electric\ force\ in\ Newtons$$

, in which E_v is an electric field in Volts per metre. And A = Area in square meters. A useful thing about this formula is that you do not need to specify any electric charges to get a force in newtons.

I think I read that this formula applies to the electric field in the gap between the plates of a parallel plate capacitor, and it also applies to the electric field of a radio wave, as any electromagnetic wave. In both cases energy was considered to be stored in space in the electric field. And when it is about a radio wave you assume that an equal amount of energy is stored in space by a magnetic field.

It was interesting that the same formula is also used for the magnetic energy stored in space per unit volume. A unit of area was 1 meter squared, and a unit of volume was 1 meter cubed. So this equation can mean two things, either force over unit area, or energy in a unit of volume, or 1 meter cubed. I think the force per area can do mechanical work over a depth, and a depth times an area produces a volume, and the mechanical work is considered to come from energy stored in space in the field itself in that volume.

$$\frac{\mu_o H^2}{2}$$ =Magnetic Force Per Unit Area, Newton = Magnetic Energy Per Unit Volume, Joules.

If the magnetic field's force were assumed to be acting over the whole surface area of a sphere (an assumption that is obviously NOT correct) then the force over the area would be in Newtons =

$$\frac{\mu_o H^2 \times 4\pi R^2}{2} = \mu_o H^2 \times 2\pi R^2$$

In the case of the spinning field, if the total of the electric field's energy plus the magnetic field's energy were evenly filling the volume of a sphere (an assumption that is NOT correct) then the total energy would be =

$$\frac{1}{2}\mu_o H^2 \times \frac{4}{3}\pi R^3 + \frac{1}{2}\epsilon_o E_v^2 \times \frac{4}{3}\pi R^3 = \mu_o H^2 \frac{4}{3}\pi R^3$$ (Assuming both the electric field and the

magnetic fields share half the total energy)

$$So\quad Centrifugal\_Force = \frac{\mu_o H^2 \times \frac{4}{3}\pi R^3}{R} = \mu_o H^2 \times \frac{4}{3}\pi R^2$$

$$\frac{Magnetic\ field\ force_{newton}}{Centrifugal\ force_{newton}} = \frac{\mu_o H^2 \times 2\pi R^2}{\mu_o H^2 \times \frac{4}{3}\pi R^2} = \frac{3}{2} = 1.5$$

The ratio of the magnetic force to the centrifugal force is therefore not affected by the radius or by the total energy, or by the field strength. It seems to be a fixed ratio of 1.5x. I get exactly the same result when calculating for the electric field.

This is not intended to be an accurate calculation, it is only a very rough approximate calculation because it assumes several things which are not correct: In reality the fields would not be uniformly spread out through the volume of a sphere, and the fields would not be acting on the whole surface area of a sphere, and the mass of ball lightning causing the centrifugal force as it is spinning, would not be completely located at the outer edge or largest radius, and you would have to first understand how forces hold it in a round ball shape and then use integration.

But the rough calculation still shows that either electric field or the magnetic field considered alone if acting over the whole area of a sphere, can be more than strong enough to overcome the centrifugal force which ball lightning has because it is spinning so quickly.
It is also interesting that the ratio of either field force divided by centrifugal force is not a variable depending on energy or size, but seems to be perhaps a constant which does not change with any of these variables.
It seems probable that even if the calculation was done more accurately, you would still find that the ratio of field force to centrifugal force is like a constant that would not be affected by changing most of the variables such as diameter and energy.
If a calculation were more accurate, I suppose the ratio might maybe be nearer to 1:1 .
 And I couldn't possibly try to calculate it accurately since I do not understand the whole reason why the ball lightning condenses into a round spinning ball.

An experiment when the equipment works.
A lot of empty space in the air is necessary for the experiment. (You would need an empty room or else to do the experiment outdoors where there is more room than indoors).

A small object should hang in the air. Either a small piece of iron wire, maybe an electro-statically charged ball can hang on the end of a thread. It should hang in the air from a cotton thread, or if it's likely to get hot, a fire proof glass fibre thread.

If the object hangs to one side of their flight path, the super-polarized waves could be attracted to it, or repelled away from it. When a small piece of magnetized iron wire simply hangs from a thread at one side of the flight path of super-polarised waves, some proportion of the energy will go to orbit in complete circles around it, and continue to circle around it, spinning.

If you think of what might happen very very quickly, a curved flight path could turn into circles, and these would spiral getting smaller and smaller until rapidly a round spinning field is there.
 The field could contract until in a moment it would be very much like natural ball-lightning, forming a round spherical spinning field which spins on its axis at the speed of light.
A powerful glowing field identical to natural ball-lighting would form around a weakly magnetized piece of iron wire, which is intended to start it off, and more and more of the identical super-polarised waves or half cycles would add their energy and that is like constructive interference.
A nylon fishing line might melt, so you might have to use a fire-proof glass fibre string instead.

Now assuming that the equipment described is simply turned around 90 degrees on its side, so that the super-polarised waves have a horizontal electric field always pointing to the right, and therefore have a magnetic North and South side above and below. In that case your piece of magnetized iron wire can be vertical in the air rather than horizontal.

Obviously when the piece of iron wire is hanging from a thread on the right hand side of the beam, the spinning field which might form around it would have a clockwise rotation (looking downwards). And when the piece of iron wire is hanging at the left hand side of the beam the spinning field that forms would have an anti-clockwise rotation. But if the piece of iron wire was hanging right in the middle of the beam, then nothing would happen as that couldn't form a spinning field. Because the field probably can't have both clockwise spin and counter-clockwise spin at the same time.

It would be convenient to use a fishing rod, or a long pole. I suppose you could hang the short piece of magnetized iron wire from the end of a fishing line, and use a fishing rod to hang it where you want it, on either side of the beam of super-polarised waves. A powerful ball-lighting could immediately form around the piece of iron wire, and that experiment would work over and over very reliably.

So you would have an interesting experiment, hang the short piece of magnetized iron wire in the air with a thread from fishing rod, to one side of the beam of super-polarized waves, and see a bright ball of lighting form immediately around it. And then, you can move the ball lightning where you want it simply by handling the fishing rod. The ball lightning should continue to exist for a few minutes after all the electrical equipment is completely switched off, as ball lightning is a field which stores a lot of energy of its own. And I believe natural ball lightning sometimes lasts a few minutes.

With two fishing rods you can make two balls of lightning and bring the two together to see what happens when they meet. They could explode when they meet, depending on whether they have the same spin direction or opposite spins. In the explosion some free-floating balls of lightning might be formed which might shoot off or float quite on their own in the air. Bringing a plain piece of iron wire to meet a ball lightning could also cause an explosion, in which some of the energy of the ball-lightning could attempt to wrap itself around the second piece of iron wire, and in which some of its energy could turn back into radio waves with a bang.

Where its energy turns back into radio waves with a bang, there are two processes, it can either cease to go in circles and go off in straight lines, or the whole thing could vibrate and that could emit radio waves?

About a natural case.

In the case of natural ball lightning it is only necessary for the lightning to emit a one cycle long radio wave, and necessary for avalanche breakdown in the air to stop and absorb the energy of the second half-cycle, while the first half cycle of that radio wave flew through the air without being stopped. The natural ball-lighting is then formed from that single number 1 half-cycle of the radio wave.

In the case of natural ball-lightning it may not be necessary for more to get added together in the superimposition which is of constructive interference, because the lightning strike has such an enormous current of millions of amperes, that a radio wave pulse gets produced in which a single half-cycle has a lot of energy, enough energy on its own.

In the case of natural ball-lighting, you can calculate the sense of the induction rules to see that it makes perfect sense to assume that the first half-cycle could go through the air unhindered, and that the second half-cycle causes an avalanche breakdown in the air which then stops it and absorbs the energy of the second half-cycle.

(The air at a thunder storm would break-down more easily in one direction than in the other, because a strong electrostatic field is already in a vertical direction across it. So for an instant the air in a storm could act like the one-way window. As the natural lightning makes a radio wave, the large electric field of the radio waves' first half-cycle, would not be enough to provoke breakdown in the transparent air because it is in the opposite direction to the direction of the static electric field which is already there across the air.

But the second half-cycle would have an electric field which is in the same direction as the static electric field which is already across the air, and the sum of the radio wave electric field plus the static electric field which is already there, would provoke a breakdown in the air, absorbing the energy of the second half-cycle. So a one-way window effect happens, and gas breakdown is doing it instead of microwave semiconductors.)

If we assume that every part of a round spinning field always moves at exactly the speed of light, then the inner parts of the round spinning field would do more turns per second than the outer parts of it. Anyway it would rotate at about 100 Million to 2 Billion revolutions a second. The glowing light is probably caused by the air molecules being excited by vibrations caused by its spinning.

The ball shaped spinning field could be a glowing ball lightning if it's strong,, or totally invisible when it's not so powerful or maybe sometimes when it's totally balanced so there are no vibrations. A spinning field does not need to be perfectly balanced. It could be a bit stronger on one side than on the other. In most cases the field is not totally balanced, and the imbalance as it spins at hundreds of millions of turns a second would vibrate and the vibrations can stimulate air molecules to make them glow.

Is the angular momentum absolutely tiny?

As a ball lightning must be spinning at about 200 million to 2 billion turns a second, it could look as though it is spinning and you could surely see some gyroscopic effects when you try to turn its axis. How strong would its gyroscopic effects be??

The super-polarised waves which to begin with were radio wave half cycles, always have a small amount of momentum, just as radio waves and light waves do have a really tiny momentum. In the spinning field, the super-polarised waves might have a tiny amount of mass according to Einstein's equation E=MC square. M can be in kilograms and C in meters per second, and the result E in Joules.

An angular momentum is equal to normal momentum MV multiplied by the perpendicular distance from it to the centre of rotation. I think I understand, that the perpendicular distance R metres from the motion vector to a point which can be thought of as a centre of rotation, is like the arm of a lever. And the longer it is the better the leverage. And so the angular momentum is MVR, or normal momentum times the perpendicular distance.

If the mass of a ball-lighting was 1 microgram, this is 1 billionth of a kilogram. Its energy would be 300,000,000 squared/divided by 1 billion. Since the speed of light is 300,000,000 meters per second. C^2 is 90,000,000,000,000,000. So a mass of 1 billionth of a kilo, or a microgram is equal to 90,000,000 Joules of energy, or 90 mega-joules.

This shows that a ball lightning with 90 mega-joules energy must have a mass of 1 microgram. That sort of ball lightning would be much too powerful to make, so suppose instead you made ball lightning with a mass of 0.01 micrograms. And then its energy would be 0.9 mega-joules. Which is the same as the energy of 100 Kilowatts power charging up for 9 seconds.

An equivalent to a mass of 0.01 micrograms moving at 300,000,000 meters per second has the same momentum as a mass of 1 gram moving at 3 meters per second. This shows that a ball-lighting which has an energy of 0.9 mega-joules will have about the same momentum as it spins as a mass of 1 gram moving at 3 meters per second. If you imagine a plastic ball weighing 1 gram and turning so its surface moves at 3 meters per second, I suppose its gyroscopic forces would be about equal, and of course that is not much!

Not much at all, and it seems to me that even though centrifugal force of ball lightning can be very strong, angular momentum can only be very weak.

In a calculation, its mass M in MVR is decreased by C^2 because of $M=\dfrac{E}{C^2}$ while centripetal acceleration in metres per second per second = $\dfrac{C^2}{R}$ is increased by C^2 and the result is a centripetal force proportional to its total energy divided by its radius, and that is quite strong. However, it seems that angular momentum MVR is extremely small. I suppose it is so very very tiny because Velocity is to the 1 power? It is so small as in this case with V to the 1 power = C to the 1 power in MVR, while the mass M in MVR gets decreased by C^2 the square of the speed of light. And so angular momentum seems to be very very small compared to centrifugal force.

In fact it seems that in proportions, its angular momentum is a whole C times tinier than its centrifugal force. So it is 300,000,000 times tinier than centrifugal force.
 So gyroscopic forces in a ball-lighting of 0.9 mega-joules energy could be of similar strength to the gyroscopic effects in a ball weighing only 1 gram and turning at only about 10 turns a second.

What about the centrifugal force? How strong is it? In a spinning object centrifugal and centripetal forces are equal and opposite. Centripetal force is mass times the centripetal acceleration, that is the acceleration always pointing to the centre of the circle, which is what keeps something moving in a circle. In this case the force in Newtons must be $\dfrac{E}{C^2} x \dfrac{C^2}{R} = \dfrac{Energy}{Radius}$

The acceleration $\dfrac{C^2}{R}$ is such a very high number, if R = 0.1 metres, the acceleration is
$\dfrac{C^2}{0.1} = 9 x \dfrac{10^{16}}{0.1} = 9 x 10^{17}$ metres per second per second, or about 10^{17} times greater than the Earth's gravity.

The ball-lighting might weigh only 0.01 micrograms, but while it spins at 300,000,000 meters per second the C^2 is extremely high.

The momentum MV of 0.01 micrograms moving at 300,000,000 meters per second would be the same as the momentum of 1 gram moving at 3 meters per second.
A spinning ball 10 centimetres in radius and with its surface moving at the speed of light needs a centripetal acceleration of $\dfrac{V^2}{R} = \dfrac{C^2}{0.1} = 9 x \dfrac{10^{16}}{0.1} = 9 x 10^{17}$ meters per second per second.

Which is about 10^{17} G's. About 10^{17} times the Earth's gravity acceleration. At that acceleration 0.01 micrograms mass would need a force of $9 x 10^{17}$ x 10^{--11} = 9,000,000 Newtons of force. Which is about 900 Tonnes of force!
$C^2 = 9 x 10^{16}$ Again suppose the ball lightning is 20 centimetres in diameter, and has equivalent to the mass of 0.01 micrograms, or $10^{-11} Kg$. $M \dfrac{V^2}{R} = 10^{-11} \dfrac{(300,000,000)^2}{0.1} = 10^{-11} \dfrac{9 x 10^{16}}{0.1} =$ 9,000,000 N.

Isn't it amazing that such a tiny, tiny mass can have a 90 Tonnes centrifugal force, just because it is spinning quickly! Again assuming that a mass of 0.01 micrograms were 900 Kilo Joules.

So I think the angular momentum is very tiny, and yet I think that should not make it difficult to believe that the ball lightning should spin for a long time before it is stopped. Because, a radio wave travelling through space also has a tiny momentum, and yet though its momentum is so tiny it can keep on going for light years.

Something about rare natural ball lightning.

The necessary conditions in the air a short distance away from the bolt of lightning would be a vertical electric field across the air which is fairly close to being strong enough to cause a breakdown of the air. And, a radio wave emitted by lightning has to have a first half cycle with an electric field in the other direction, so that it will never cause breakdown.

The second half-cycle of the radio wave of course has an electric field in the opposite direction to the first half cycle. And when the second half cycle of the radio wave reaches an area of the air that is near to breakdown, the sum of the electric field of the radio wave, plus the static electric field that is already there because of the weather conditions, needs to cause an avalanche breakdown in the air that makes the air conducting of electricity and that completely stops or reflects the second half cycle.

 Now electrically conducting, the air stops any more half cycles after the first one which got through. The product produced by that whole event is a single half cycle, the leading half cycle of the radio wave, now independent and on its own. It would in the right conditions swirl around and spin and a spinning field forms which in most cases will not have much energy and can be invisible. It is made from the single radio waves' half cycle which has become isolated and on its own when the half cycles that followed it were reflected, absorbed, removed by avalanche breakdown of the air.

The spinning field would in most cases be completely transparent and invisible. But in a small proportion of cases when this happens the spinning ball will have enough energy to stimulate air molecules into emitting light.

A slight unevenness in the strength of the field as it spins at about a hundred million to 4 billion revolutions per second, stimulates molecules in the air to make a glow.

;------------------------------------

A Splitting Apart of Normal Microwaves

The next drawing is assumed to be inside a transparent spinning field.
The drawing shows a normal low power microwave which you assume has entered the spinning field. (flying from left to right.)
The normal lower power microwave is suddenly split apart into two parts, two diverging trails.

The splitting resembles somewhat a Calcite crystal and its splitting apart of a light ray, into two rays, called the normal ray and the extraordinary ray, as light enters a Calcite crystal and passes through it. A Calcite crystal refracts different polarizations different amounts.

The splitting caused by a the spinning field of ball lightning, is a more profound thing. The type of polarization is quite different from the one achieved by the Calcite crystal. And the kind of splitting is different, as the two rays are like DC waves, and they are super-polarized.

The extent of polarization in this case is twice as much as the usual plane polarization and the change is therefore more profound, so that it is not quite "a waveform" any longer, after it has split up it has no actual wavelength, and in a vaguely figurative way it is comparable to a little gust of wind.

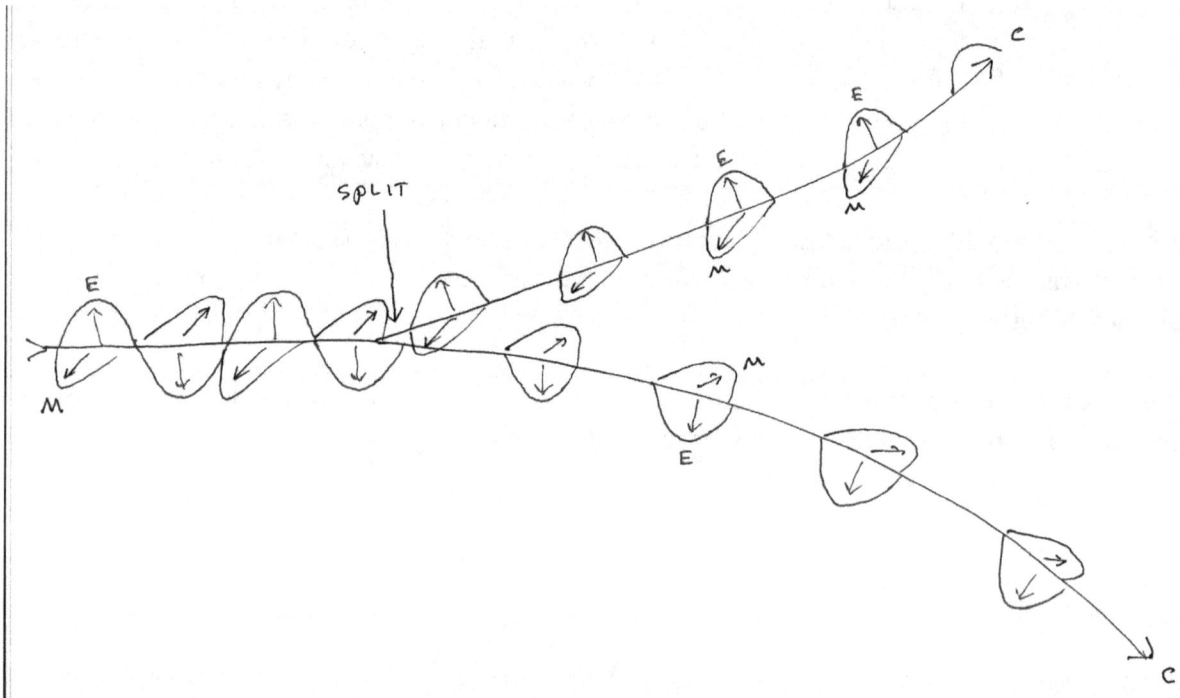

The Catalytic Property, compared to calcite

The spinning field which is closely related to ball lightning should have a catalytic property. The catalytic property would have many uses, including that it would make something invisible to radar.

Such a spinning field can easily be invisible if its power is below the level which makes the air glow with light, and for experiments about this catalytic property it should be enough to work with these invisible low powered fields. The catalytic property should be that it can split apart microwaves which have a somewhat lower energy than its own.

And one could demonstrate the catalytic property by taking a small hand-held radar gun, of the kind that is used to measure the speed of cars on roads.

You would need to hang a tiny bar magnet from the end of a string, and create around it a ball lightning which is too low in energy to be visible.

The invisible spinning field might not be seen, but, assume that the small bar magnet is normally clearly visible on radar. If not you could also place some crumpled up aluminium foil somewhere right behind the spinning field, so that the foil should normally be visible to the hand-held radar.

As soon as the invisible or barely visible spinning field forms in the air around the small magnet, it should become invisible on the radar. Radar will no longer see a reflection from it or from foil which you placed right behind it.

What should happen is that when the normal lower powered microwaves from the hand held radar begin to enter the spinning field, those microwaves are split apart. And they are split up into more of super-polarized waves, which can also be called separated half-cycles. This splitting apart is vaguely comparable to the splitting of normal light rays by a Calcite crystal, except that in this case the split rays cease to be visible on radar as they are no longer microwaves after being split.

The normal microwaves should be split up into two trails of super-polarized waves, these two rays a same type field as the spinning field itself. So you could say that the spinning field creates more of itself, by splitting up a microwave into something that is like its own self.

One trail would be repelled and pushed away from the spinning field. The other trail will be joining the spinning field and probably becoming part of it. When the normal microwave enters the spinning field and gets split apart into two parts, the part which has the same field orientation as the spinning field will join it. While the part which has an opposite field direction is repelled away from it, and they are split apart.

The factors which could increase the amount of splitting? Firstly the spinning field needs to be stronger in field force than the microwaves that come into it. A second factor must be the radius of curvature of the spinning field, as if the spinning field is small in diameter, it would split microwaves more than a wider field.

This is the catalytic property by which super-polarized waves in a spinning field can create more of their own kind. But it happens without an increase in energy, on the contrary splitting a normal microwave apart should use up a slight amount of energy.

Daniel H. Rosenthal   my email: danielrosenthal66@yahoo.com